VIDA BLUE
COMING UP AGAIN

by Don Kowet

77- 8143

G. P. Putnam's Sons • **New York**

Second Impression

Contents

1   A Gift and a Guideline   **9**

2   Knowing What Oblivion Is   **21**

3   The Minors   **32**

4   Capturing Control   **48**

5   Star or Comet?   **62**

6   What Good Is a Cadillac?

7   Mounting Pressure   **85**

8   No Peace Anywhere   **95**

9   Losing the Play-off   **101**

10   Playing It Cool   **106**

11   Oh, Charlie O.!   **114**

12   Also a Man   **121**

13   Struggle for Survival   **127**

14   A Changed Vida Blue   **145**

Index   **157**

VIDA BLUE
COMING UP AGAIN

1

A Gift and a Guideline

The year was 1966. Vida Blue was seventeen, a six-foot, 180-pound quarterback at DeSoto High School, who'd thrown thirty-five touchdown passes in fourteen games to carry his team to a district football championship. So football was on his mind. Football, meaning four years strolling across a neat landscaped campus. He would attend classes, washed by the flattering glances of pretty co-eds. He would play football and make a future for himself.

"I was going to quarterback the Baltimore Colts," he recalls. "I was going to be the black Johnny Unitas. I could see myself standing behind one of those big pro lines, calling audibles. . . . I was a roll-out quarterback, a drop-back quarterback, and a scrambler. I did it all."

Baseball seemed less of a challenge. It lacked dramatic appeal. In the drowsy northwest Louisiana mill town of Mansfield (population 10,000), about 20 miles from Shreveport, every boy coordinated enough to snatch a ball in midflight took to baseball as naturally as black city kids grew up with basketball. Equipment? The tin-shanty or clapboard houses—paint flaking under a relentless summer sun—lacked central heating. So there were always stacks of firewood—stray branches to serve for bats. Vida Blue's father worked a steady, if dreary, job at a local mill, so there was always cash on hand to buy some kind of ball. And even when the money came hard, Vida had his baseballs.

"Vida was just a boy when his grandfather—my father—gave me a piece of advice," recalls Vida's mother, Sallie Blue. "He told me: 'Someday that boy's gonna be a great baseball player. If you're smart, you'll keep him in baseballs. Every time he wants a ball you go out to the store and get him one.'" Mrs. Blue adds with a smile, "And I did."

Vida was born on July 28, 1949, in the same wood-frame house he grew up in. The house was located on Mary Street—downtown Mansfield in the heart of the black ghetto. Vida was the first of six children. In celebration of the event, his father insisted that the child be named Vida—*life* in Spanish. And the name was both a gift and a guideline.

Vida Blue, Sr., in his early thirties when his first son and namesake was born, had been raised on the farmlands surrounding the town. At an early age, Vida Senior's family had left the parched land to come to

Mansfield, where factories had begun to sprout. From his teens, Vida Senior had been employed at a steel foundry. Year after year he'd burned the fat off his body, turned wiry and thin enduring stifling furnace heat to convert molten steel into chains and miles of pipe and buckets. It was a living wage, but barely. And the only alternative in Mansfield was boring, menial work in a garment factory.

So he gave his son his name, thereby conferring upon him life and a challenge to life. "You got to *do* something with your life," he told his son from the time Vida could understand. "You gotta move on and move up in this world."

Vida grew to the spirit of his name. "He was an active baby," recalls Sallie Blue, "always grabbing for things, and trying to stand up before his legs were ready to hold him. He wasn't one of those kids who're always crying and cranky. He was laughing from the beginning, using that smile of his to charm everyone around."

Vida. Life. From infancy his characteristic trait was an irrepressible vitality. He was clever; he used his cleverness to get around adults, conning them with a smile or a piece of innocent flattery. Sometimes his inordinate energy led him into mischief. By the time he entered school for the first time, he had countless broken windows to his credit—usually the result of a thrown or batted baseball. Countless little girls had had their long braids yanked by Vida Blue. Countless expeditions into forbidden backyards had been logged. At school, he was never destructive, merely playful.

And in Southern schools in rural black ghettos fifteen years ago, an intelligent child *had* to resort to mischief to shatter the unending boredom.

Of course, Vida's school was all black. Although teachers trained in state colleges were competent and willing, facilities were primitive. When black children entered school for the first time, they were suddenly confronted with a foreign culture. And what good, after all, would schooling do them? There was no money at home for a college education and therefore no pressure put on the child to work toward one. Thus, for Vida and the other kids from his neighborhood, school was viewed as an unavoidable fact of life, a compulsory ten-year prison term, whose dullness could be alleviated only by laughter.

One day when he was in the eighth grade, Vida arrived at his classroom before his teacher. His body hidden from the waist down to his classmates, he bent over behind his teacher's desk, then returned, chuckling, to his seat. Soon the teacher entered. She greeted the children, and sat down—then straight up, with a damnation in her mouth and a bottom full of tacks.

Vida could have lied; he could have escaped punishment. But when the teacher demanded to know who had laid the tack trap, Vida immediately confessed. After all, it was the kind of prank he had seen in comic books, Dennis the Menace type behavior which leads to OUCHES!, but no real damage. He was shocked now. He hadn't realized that pain can come from converting a thoughtless fantasy into action.

But despite the fact that he'd pleaded guilty, the

school administration took quick action—and this time the pain was Vida's. He was kicked off the basketball team for the rest of the year. And Vida Blue had been the star of that basketball team. And where Vida Blue came from, sports were king.

Sports play a very important role in black ghettos, North or South. Sure, black kids play cowboys and Indians. But it's not a very satisfying game for them because there's no one to identify with. Historians have ignored the blacks who contributed to the development of the West. Black kids have no Wyatt Earps, Buffalo Bills, Billy the Kids to use as heroic models for their fantasies. In fact, until recently, the only way blacks figured in the history books they read at school was as slaves.

However, since the late forties, when Jackie Robinson broke the color bar in the National League, followed by Larry Doby three months later in the American League, black kids could be proud of their athletes—disadvantaged kids whose ability and determination had brought them money, fame, and the respect of the white community. Louisiana has been a particularly fertile breeding ground for black athletes, owing in part to athletic programs developed at Southern University at Baton Rouge, whose basketball team has fed ballplayers like the Chicago Bulls' All-Star forward Bob Love into the NBA and whose baseball program produced the Atlanta Braves' Ralph Garr. Grambling College at Grambling, Louisiana, has consistently developed football players destined to star in the National Football League. So Vida's play fantasies drifted to sports, whose heroes were of the same background, class—and skin color.

Every day after school, Vida and his friends covered the distance home at a quick trot, put down their books, and gulped a midday snack. Throwing their school clothes helter-skelter around their rooms—rooms they inevitably shared with brothers or sisters—they picked up battered hand-me-down baseball gloves and a chipped bat with the name of some current star engraved on it (or in other seasons a weather-beaten football or basketball). A half hour after the final school bell rang, they were out on the empty lot near the Blues' house—a tribe of Henry Aarons, Willie Mayeses, Bob Gibsons in miniature, arguing over a close call at the piece of wood that served for third base.

Football season was Vida's favorite, for then he was suddenly transformed from an insignificant Mansfield ghetto kid into an NFL quarterback—a black Johnny Unitas, scrambling away from clutching hands to let loose with a long pass that brought 100,000 fans to their feet. . . .

But his grammar school had no football team. At school he played only basketball and softball. It was there he got his only coaching in sports. He listened; he learned. While basketball and softball were irrelevant to his quarterbacking dreams, despite himself, his body responded and he excelled.

Baseball, though, was what he knew best. In the fourth grade he had joined a local Little League team.

He could hit as well as anybody, run and field with the best. But in Little League, as in major-league baseball, the crucial position is pitcher—and Vida Blue had the best arm for his age in Mansfield. From the beginning, he was fast. As he got taller, his fast ball blazed harder. By the time he entered high school his arm had earned a reputation.

"Vida, he can really burn that thing," the kids used to whisper as they watched him throw at the DeSoto High School athletic field. Unfortunately, the rest of the local towns were unable to put his reputation to the test. For the future big-league superstar had the misfortune to attend a high school that didn't have a baseball team; DeSoto High was primarily a football school. Thus, Vida Blue, whose talent lay in his arm, naturally thought of passing a football, not pitching a baseball, as the stepping-stone to local fame.

The emphasis on football to the exclusion of baseball ended the summer of Vida's twelfth year. One day the umpire of a Little League game Vida was scheduled to pitch in suddenly took sick. As a replacement, DeSoto's football coach, Clarence Baldwin, agreed to stand in as umpire. By another stroke of fate, DeSoto High's principal, Lee Jacobs, just happened to be a spectator.

Blue began to pitch, depending from the outset on his only weapon—a burning fast ball. With Umpire Baldwin behind the plate, for the first two innings Vida threw fast ball after fast ball, and every one a strike. But at the end of two innings, although he hadn't given up a single hit, his team was losing, 2–0. Why? His catcher had as much trouble holding onto Vida's pitches as the batters had hitting them.

Disgusted, at the end of that second inning Vida ran off the mound and threw his glove down at his feet. His catcher came over to him apologetically and said, "I just can't hold 'em anymore. I'm sorry. I can't stop 'em, 'cause you throwin' so hard my hand's gone and swelled up." Baldwin, who was standing nearby, overheard the conversation. He spoke to Vida's coach, who then changed catchers every other inning for the rest of the game.

Vida pitched a three-hitter that day, gave up no earned runs, but still managed to lose, 2–1.

After the game coach Baldwin had a long talk with principal Jacobs. They realized that this was no ordinary arm, no ordinary talent. Yet, they mused, in a few years Vida would be too old for Little League baseball. "And we don't have a baseball team up at the high school," Lee Jacobs said.

The two men looked at each other, suddenly struck by the same thought.

"There's no rule that says we *can't* have a baseball team," said coach Baldwin after a long, thoughtful silence.

Principal Jacobs smiled. "That's true," he said. "There's no rule, and no reason why not."

By the time Vida entered DeSoto High School there *was* a baseball team, led by coach Clyde Washington. The conference in which Vida played both football and baseball at DeSoto was the Louisiana Interscholastic Athletic and Literary Organization, the exotic "Literary" reference owing to the fact that debating teams also competed. The LIALO was black only and was later disbanded when the Supreme Courts' "desegregate or else" dictum finally filtered down to Mansfield.

Vida entered DeSoto High in the fall of 1964 as a sophomore. (Mansfield has junior high schools.) He had now grown to his full six feet in height and weighed about 180. Beside his incredible throwing arm, his best natural asset for sports was his legs—which could carry him, he says, 100 yards in 9.8 seconds. Although he had starred in basketball in grammar school and junior high, his interest was still football (not baseball) and becoming the "black Johnny Unitas." All he had to do now was entice his football coaches at DeSoto into the fantasy.

Even though he was only fifteen and a first-year man, it was obvious from the opening day of football practice that Vida would make the varsity and at a starting position. The only question was where. Yes, he could throw a football 65 yards with uncanny accuracy and blinding speed. But he could run, too. He was tall and agile. He had big, sure hands and looked like a natural end. Eventually, his coaches told each other, he'd be able to move in at quarterback. But could a fifteen-year-old kid fresh out of junior high guide the team's offense *now?*

The coaches decided to gamble. When the varsity squad list was posted, fifteen-year-old Vida Blue was first-string quarterback.

The first game that year, against Webster High, would be Vida Blue's test—the first time, in fact, that his dream of becoming a pro quarterback would submit to the pressure-cooker reality of a game situation.

But Vida proved he had poise to match his precocious physical development. With a short twisting scamper here, a roll-out pass there, Vida led his team to a 20–7 shellacking of Webster, DeSoto's three touchdowns coming off Vida Blue passes. Vida also proved that his legs were as accurate and sure as his arm. Handling DeSoto's punting chores, he twice kicked for more than 60 yards, angling one punt to trap Webster back at its own 2-yard line.

For those who still needed convincing that he had the physical *and* mental maturity to quarterback, Vida provided Saturday after Saturday of conclusive proof. He led DeSoto to the conference championship in only his first year on the varsity.

But when baseball season rolled around, the problem was not whether Vida could pitch, but who would catch him. Coach Washington did have two senior catchers who were willing—and for the most part able—to withstand the battering their hands would take as targets for Vida's fast ball. Anyway, Vida would pitch only about half of his team's games, so the catcher who last caught him would have a chance to soak the swelling out of his hand before his next assignment.

With two catchers available to trap the blistering fast ball after Vida struck out his hapless opponents, DeSoto breezed to the 1964–65 conference championship.

At the same time, coach Washington began to work with sophomore catcher Elijah Williams. Throughout the 1964–65 season, Washington and his assistant coaches tried to turn Williams into a catcher who could handle Vida for the next two years until he graduated.

Williams managed his game-time chores with no difficulty. He had an accurate arm and sure hands. But as soon as he faced Vida in practice (coach Washington never let him catch Blue in league games), his hands reacted the same way everyone else's had to Vida's fast ball—with blisters.

Coach Washington's solution was to purchase a heavy pair of work gloves, cut the fingers off the left glove, and order Williams to wear it under his catcher's mitt—already bloated with extra padding. This raised Williams' level of tolerance for pain an additional two innings.

Next Washington added a sponge lining to the mitt —and with his left hand bulging with thick glove, sponge lining, and extra padding, Elijah Williams was given his first starting assignment with Vida Blue on the mound. Williams managed to endure the entire seven-inning game, but when Elijah awoke the next morning, his hand had swollen to the size of a small grapefruit.

Coach Washington had learned his lesson. The next season, 1965–66, with his two senior backstops gone, Vida pitched only one of every three games. And Williams caught only when Vida pitched—the whole rotative syndrome having been devised to allow Williams' hand sufficient time to deflate down to its normal size between Blue's pitching stints.

But one sure victory out of every three games was again a secure enough margin to assure a second straight conference title for DeSoto.

2

Knowing What Oblivion Is

By his senior year in high school Vida's performance
on the diamond had converted his grandfather's predic-
tion into prophecy. Vida began the year as captain of
the football team. In fourteen games, he threw for two
miles of total yardage through the air. (Although a
natural southpaw, he was coordinated enough on roll-
outs to throw right-handed for short yardage.) DeSoto's
final game of the season was against traditional rival
Booker T. Washington High School of Shreveport. And
this year Booker was fielding a group of mammoths
whose steamrolling line play made them prohibitive
favorites.

The first quarter was a standoff, with the Booker T.
backs controlling the ball behind their monstrous
front line, and the DeSoto attack smothered by Booker
T.'s awesome defensive front four. But each time the

21

boys from Booker T. got dangerously near the DeSoto goal line, they were stopped. And Vida Blue managed to punt for good position and out of danger.

With only minutes left in the quarter, Vida dropped back, rolled to his left, and unleashed a 40-yard touchdown pass to a teammate who had sliced through the secondary into the end zone. DeSoto converted the extra point, and the quarter ended with DeSoto on top, 7–0.

Rain began to fall in the second quarter, but Vida managed to control the slippery ball for a 30-yard touchdown pass that made the score 13–0. The rain fell in torrents through the half-time pause, and when the third quarter began, Vida was under strict instructions to stick to the ground.

So weather had accomplished what the hard rush of the Booker T. defensive line couldn't—and the passing arm of Vida Blue was curtailed as effectively as if someone had broken it. But a tremendous effort by the De-Soto defense stopped the Booker T. rushing game cold. Meanwhile, DeSoto played its own kind of ball control game—which meant that Vida Blue carried the football on every single play from the beginning of the second half until the final whistle. DeSoto didn't score again, but Blue ate up so much game time with his power sprints to the outside, his snakelike lunges between guard and tackle, that the kids from Booker T. had a piece of Vida Blue in their hands more often than they had the ball.

DeSoto finally won, 13–0. Vida Blue relaxed on the team bus en route back to Mansfield. He felt good,

really good. He had played his final game of high
school football, and the stands had been full of college
scouts. The first leg of his climb toward glory as a black
Unitas was completed.

Ironically, he never for one moment imagined that
this, his hour of triumph as a football player, would
also mark his final hour of gridiron competition.

When he wasn't quarterbacking, of course, he was
pitching. Even then he had the high leg kick, the knack
for hiding that left hand behind his hip as he rocked
back, his body becoming a disarming yawn, until he
came down hard off the mound with a fast ball that was
by in a blink. In one seven-inning game he struck out
twenty-one batters. That year he again pitched DeSoto
High to a district championship.

But baseball was second best. There were black
pitchers aplenty throughout the big leagues, yet no
starting black quarterbacks. So baseball lacked challenge. And glamor. Baseball players graduated from
high school into minor-league farm systems—towns a
thousand miles from Mansfield, but just as poor, with
accommodations in third-rate hotels, with travel between games in battered station wagons, to play in
two-bit ball parks for two-timing owners. It promised
no leap from DeSoto High to campus Saturdays with
30,000 out to see you throw that magnificent last-
minute touchdown pass.

For most a ticket to the minors is a one-way pass to
oblivion. And Vida already knew oblivion. He was
born black, born poor, born invisible.

"Sure we all had uniforms back in Mansfield," he recalled later, with that characteristic dry humor. "A white T-shirt, a pair of blue jeans."

In football, though, he had that shiny plastic helmet, the stiff Clark Kent shoulder pads, the strip of convex face mask that made everyone equal by obliterating facial distinctions. Football was class. Football was like chivalric knights engaged in ritual combat. A Johnny Unitas was all brain, all skill, a subtle master lording it over loyal and aggressive drones. Now that was class. Vida Blue class!

And then came that day in 1968 when the "impossible" happened. Vida Blue's father—the dependable breadwinner, the just arbiter of disputes among his two sons and four daughters, the tall man with wiry arms muscled like sailors' rope—Vida Blue, Sr., died of a heart attack.

"When it happened," says Sallie Blue, "I told Junior [Vida's childhood nickname]: 'Now you're the man of the house.' "

Everything was different now. Dream busted. No black Johnny Unitas. No Baltimore Colt uniform. No money and seven mouths to feed.

"My daddy's death made me grow up overnight," Vida says. "All of a sudden I looked around and the man in the family was me!"

One day Vida was a carefree seventeen-year-old— tall, good-looking, a magnet for co-eds' affection, a high school superstar with an ambitious goal and the talent to achieve it. Then, suddenly, he was head of a household in dire economic straits. Yes, he could still inch toward his "black Johnny Unitas" dream. Offers were flocking in from everywhere. More than 100 colleges and universities across the nation contacted him; twenty-five colleges offered him firm football scholarships. The University of Houston wanted to make him the first black quarterback at a major Southwestern school. Nearby Grambling wanted him. Notre Dame and Purdue submitted firm bids.

Vida could have left the family to its own devices and opted for a four-year preparatory course to pro football. His decision would test not only his attachment to his family, but Vida's very character. He could always have justified his choice of four years at college as "best for the family in the long run."

But there was another fact of life to consider now that he had been suddenly thrust into manhood. The traditional pro bias against black quarterbacks, he realized, was a stumbling block he might not be able to hurdle, no matter how great his talent. It was conceivable that he might start for four years in college at quarterback, yet never get a fair shot at the position with the pros. Furthermore, he was aware of the possibility of injury—crippling, perhaps—somewhere along the line to stardom. Although the average careers of a pro football or pro baseball player last roughly 4.5 years, the limiting factor in the National Football League is more often injury than talent.

So, despite the firm scholarship offers, Vida was overcome with doubts about making a career in football. In retrospect, of course, his decision to opt for baseball over football had been made the day his father died. But Vida was still considering his options—still thought he had options to consider—when the Kansas City Athletics picked him on the second round of the free-agent draft.

The colleges weren't the only ones who had been scouting Vida over the past two years. Word of his amazing fast ball had drifted up from the high school league to the files of major-league ball clubs. Numerous clubs were building up dossiers on the seventeen-year-old sensation. Scouts in the area were making sudden and unaccustomed side trips to Mansfield to watch Blue pitch.

Periodically he would notice them. Stepping back off the rubber between pitches, lifting his cap to rub the sweat off his forehead, then wipe it on his cap, he'd see white men, middle-aged mostly, unassuming types with the heavy-jowled, thick but slope-shouldered torsos of ex-athletes slowly going to fat. Nothing unusual about them—except at the eyes, which were shrewd, piercing —the eyes of a professional horse trader out to buy a stallion at a bargain. From time to time—if there were two of them—one would lean over to the other and whisper something. The other scout would nod his head in agreement. And neither one would have taken his eyes off Vida Blue.

After a while Vida stopped looking for them. He came to accept the fact that in every game he pitched he'd be judged by scouts. His senior year, though, after the death of his father, he took a new interest in them.

The day DeSoto played Central High (from a town called Natchitoches, some 60 miles away), the scout in attendance was Jack Sanford of the Kansas City Athletics, reputed to have the sharpest pair of eyes for young diamond talent in the country. Vida was pitching, Elijah Williams was behind the plate, ready again to offer up his hand in ritual sacrifice to the Blue fast ball.

On this day it was worth the pain Elijah would endure tomorrow. Vida's fast ball was smoking as it never had before. With scout Jack Sanford in bug-eyed disbelief in the stands, Vida Blue struck out every Central High batter who dared step into the batters' box. Twenty-one men in a row either swung blindly at Vida's pitches or stood with their bats glued to their shoulders, vainly trying to locate the guided missile that the young left-hander was launching. Besides pitching a no-hit, no-walk, no-contest 1–0 victory, Vida also blasted a double to drive home DeSoto's winning run.

It was an amazing exhibition of pure pitching power. Scout Sanford wasted no time after the game. Returning to his hotel, he immediately placed a long-distance call to Charles O. Finley.

"The kid's incredible," Sanford told the A's owner breathlessly. "And they say he's only lost two games here ever, and both of those because the catchers couldn't hold onto his fast ball. Incredible," Sanford repeated, still unable to digest mentally the performance he had witnessed that afternoon.

And Charles O. Finley was listening.

Since Blue was Kansas City's first choice, owner Charlie Finley decided to personally telephone Mansfield to sign him. The death of Vida's father had been the first damper to Vida's dreams of football glory. In his sudden indecision about his future, the facts of NFL life—its bias against black quarterbacks—had generated more doubts. Thus, into this chaotic moment of Vida Blue's life, when he seemed to be pulled along in a hundred directions at once, his dream in conflict with the obvious needs of his present reality, stepped Charles O. Finley, one of the most controversial figures ever to enter American sport.

Finley was born in Birmingham, Alabama, and it was there that the double strands of his fate were woven—baseball and salesmanship. He's fond of recalling how, while still in grammar school, he won a medal and a bicycle by selling 12,500 copies or subscriptions to the *Saturday Evening Post.*

He became a batboy for the Birmingham Barons of the American Association. Later he went on to semipro ball, played first base until he was twenty-nine, then sponsored two semipro teams and a Little League club. In 1960, through supersalesmanship unlike anything major-league sports had seen before, he managed to raise $4,000,000 to bail out the group of Kansas City businessmen who held title to the A's franchise.

He began to spend money, millions at a throw; then he began to antagonize the baseball establishment, making more enemies than friends. Later he would dazzle the world of sports by convincing the league to permit him to transport his franchise to Oakland.

Throughout, the multimillionaire had always generated a bizarre type of enthusiasm, backed up by dollars, that was bound to catalyze strong loyalties and deep abiding resentments.

One thing no detractor would deny him, though. Charlie Finley is one of the greatest salesmen this nation has ever known. And this was the man who telephoned Mansfield to convince an already-floundering seventeen-year-old that with the A's organization lay the true promise of his future.

Vida had before his father's death decided what his future plans were—at least tentatively. The University of Houston had made him the best scholarship offer to play football, and he had given his tentative agreement to its representatives. However, there was one stumbling block to be overcome before he could matriculate. Although a pretty good student at DeSoto, Vida had failed a couple of courses early on and therefore lacked sufficient credits for his high school diploma. His plan —acceptable, of course, to the recruiters from Houston —was to attend summer school after graduation to make up the necessary credits and so meet the university's entrance requirements.

But DeSoto High School was an all-black school. Southern states, with the plantation mentality still in the air 100 years after the Civil War, made no provisions for summer schools at most black high schools. And it wasn't merely because of an unconscious residue of racism. Few black students could afford *not* to work in the summers. With fathers and mothers employed at subsistence-level wages in local sweatshops or as tenant farmers eking out a meager living on local plots, children grew up knowing that it was incumbent on them to contribute something to the family income as soon as they were strong enough to perform physical labor.

Thus, Vida was forced to travel out of Mansfield, to the nearest black high school that offered a summer school program. Throughout the summer, he planned to commute to Temple High School in nearby Lorman, Mississippi.

One call from Charlie Finley changed his plans. Finley spoke with the vocabulary he had acquired in years of struggle to the top of the hierarchy of high finance. He phrased his arguments in dollars and cents. And when the conversation was over, the net worth of his persuasiveness to Vida Blue was $25,000 bonus money if he would forsake his black Unitas dream and sign to play baseball with Finley's organization.

However, Vida was cool enough under fire to tell Finley he needed a couple of days to consider the offer. He talked it over with his mother, his coaches. It was an enormous sum to a seventeen-year-old kid whose father had just died, whose mother had been left with no means of support besides the small salary she earned working at a clothing factory, and with payments due on the mortgage for their house. No one could offer arguments to refute Finley's logic of cash-on-the-line.

A few days later Finley called again. Vida told him that he would sign. His only demand was that he be allowed to attend summer school in order to obtain his high school diploma. Finley agreed, and the terms of

only recommendation was their rock-bottom rates. And even then it was effectively an overcharge for lumpy beds, windows with a permanent dirt filter, carpets beaten colorless by a thousand plodding shoes, a veritable graveyard of derelict furniture.

The meal allowances were absurd. After games on the road would come hours and hours of interminable bus rides, with pit stops for a hot dog and hamburger that you took out and ate while the bus roared on into the night.

It was a spartan life, especially for someone like Vida, who was turned off by the bright lights of local night spots.

And there were the teammates. A few, like Vida, had the promise of a future still before them. Others had sampled the spice of big-league glory. With their future now become their past, they were hanging on for a few more years, performing the only job they were qualified for.

But most of the Class A players were doomed to wander from club to club throughout their careers without ever having tasted the sweet victory of breakfast at a big-league training table. Vida's roommate at Burlington was one of them. Stan Jones had begun his career with Geneva in the New York-Pennsylvania League in 1959. Any chance he'd had of climbing out of obscurity and up toward the big leagues had been lost that year when the parent club failed to promote him even though he had compiled a 19–4 won/lost record.

Why hadn't he been promoted? Not even Stan

knows. Perhaps it was because the parent club was heavily committed that year to promote players in whom it had invested large sums of bonus monies. Perhaps the rosters of the Class AA farm teams in the organization were already stacked for that coming season. Maybe someone at Geneva passed on an off-hand remark suggesting that Stan needed another year of seasoning or that Class A was the limit of his capabilities.

For whatever reason, Stan never really got a chance to prove whether or not he had big-league potential. He became a career minor-leaguer, relegated to an overdose of obscurity in Class A ball.

When Vida joined the Bees, Stan was already twenty-eight years old, a veteran of bumpy fields, flea-infested hotels, and poverty-line food allowances. He'd been bouncing around the league for nine years now. So he shared his nine years' experience with young Vida, protecting him like an older brother from the pitfalls that can overwhelm nineteen-year-old ball-players away from home and on the road for the first time.

More important, he introduced Vida to something that had up to now completely escaped his acquaintance—the curve ball. Stan knew how to throw it; you don't last nine years in any league, whether A or Triple A or the majors, without learning how to bend your fast ball around the hitter's bats.

His pitching advice was only partially effective. Vida never really mastered the curve while at Burlington, depending—as he had in high school—for the most part on his fast ball. But the Class A ballplayers had little more luck hitting it than had the kids in the LIALO back in Louisiana.

It was here at Burlington that Vida developed another characteristic habit he was eventually to take with him to the majors. Rare is the baseball player who doesn't consider—along with his glove, spikes, and bat—a mouthful of chewing tobacco as standard game equipment. Originally a rural Southern habit, over the years baseball players from the Bronx to Bakersfield have accepted the chewing of tobacco as a necessary initiation rite into the pro world. With the age of television, ballplayers may have become more circumspect about where they empty their mouths of tobacco juice. But anyone who has walked around the inner sanctums of professional dugouts has had, inevitably, to give a quick reflex leg lift or two to avoid getting his shoes spattered.

Vida, however, couldn't stand the taste. But no ballplayer worthy of his pro status can imagine himself without jaw feverishly grinding, so he picked up the habit of stuffing his mouth with bubble gum instead. Thus came the image later captured by countless photographers when Vida came up with Oakland to stay: Vida Blue caught coming down off his high leg kick, his hand releasing the ball at the same moment as his lips were popping a giant sphere.

But that was Vida's only resemblance to the major-league sensation he'd soon become. Right now he was raw—a diamond in the rough in need of plenty of work.

Like most young fast ball pitchers, he had only the vaguest notion as to where his pitches were going. True, his wildness intimidated some batters, causing them to flinch instinctively away from the plate every time Vida kicked back off his left leg. More often than not, though, his pitch went wild, permitting a base runner to get a cheap score. Eighteen times he threw wild that season—the second-worst total in a league where to be wild is to be normal. His 80 bases on balls were also the league's second-worst total.

But he had shown speed, style, and promise—potential enough to be promoted the following season to Birmingham, Alabama, of the Southern League.

Blue made the jump from Class A Burlington to Class AA Birmingham without a hitch. The biggest change, as far as Vida was concerned, wasn't the quality of competition, but the improved quality of accommodations—and facilities in general. The teams still traveled by chartered bus, but now there was a meal allowance adequate for at least a skimpy dinner *inside* the restaurant. The ball parks even had locker rooms, so Blue could travel from his hotel in street clothes, incognito.

And there was good reason for the locker rooms. At Burlington it hadn't really mattered whether the ballplayers were seen on the streets in their uniform; no one in town really cared. Birmingham was a city of 350,000 people. The average attendance for home games was about 5,000, compared to the 500 who had watched him pitch—on a very good day—in Burlington.

The operation was more professional in every aspect. Now he wasn't sharing space on the team bus with only also-rans and has-beens. There were other ballplayers on the club with major-league potential. At Burlington, there had been no direction for a ballplayer to go but up. At Birmingham, the competition was stiffer. After all, have a bad year and you were liable to end up . . . well . . . in Burlington again.

In Vida's first start for Birmingham, he faced the Rebels of Montgomery, Alabama. It was an auspicious debut. In the first five innings he struck out nine batters, while giving up not a single run. Coasting home on a tremendous lead, Vida won, 13–3.

But Vida was soon to have his problems. If he had been a one-pitch pitcher at Burlington, at Birmingham he had only expanded his repertoire by half—a curve that sometimes broke with the abrupt angle of a hockey-stick blade, or a change-up that sometimes appeared to be moving backward, so slow did it descend off his deceptively quick arm motion.

But the key word here is "sometimes." When he was "on," he had a fast ball, curve, and change-up. When he was average, batters caught his curve before it broke, and blasted it, or teed off on a change-up that fooled no one. And some of those Double A hitters *could* hit a fast ball. Vida could still blaze his pitch by 80 percent of the league's hitters, but those other 20 percent simply waited for one in the strike zone and blasted it back at him as fast as Vida had thrown it.

Under pressure for the first time in his pitching career, Vida came temporarily unstuck. When his curve and change-up weren't working for him, he'd throw only fast balls, bearing down to the point where he lost control, sending batters sprawling into the dust in self-defense—and then down to first base as casualties hit by a pitch or on a free ride with a base on balls.

Another first for Vida—and this one a hard pill to swallow for an energetic nineteen-year-old with an irrepressible ego. For the first time in his career, early that season Vida wasn't even the No. 1 pitcher on the club. In his second outing, against Asheville, North Carolina, Blue came apart at the seams, giving up eight hits and five runs in only two and two-thirds innings. He had to be relieved by Don Boyd, who held Asheville scoreless for the rest of the game. Boyd went on to win his first four starts that year, relegating Vida to a runner-up spot as the club's top pitcher.

Gradually, though, Vida, regained his confidence. Through the careful coaching of former big-league catcher Gus Niarhos, he learned first and foremost to pace himself, to bear down when the crucial out was necessary and coast when he could afford it. He learned that whether or not his curve was breaking for him, if he threw the pitch half speed, it was sufficient to throw off the timing of most batters. He began to learn to pitch to a batter's weakness, instead of relying on his own strength—the fast ball—to see him through every situation. And what he was learning began to pay off in victories.

At Burlington he had been able to complete only 3 out of the 24 games he appeared in. At Birmingham he started 14 and completed 8. He struck out 112

batters in 104 innings. He gave up only 2 home runs,
and threw only 7 wild pitches while helping his club
to a second-place finish. His ERA was only fair—3.20
—but his ability to give up runs that didn't hurt him,
while striking out keymen in the clutch, permitted him
to compile a fine 10–3 record. He made the Southern
All-Star team. It would have been a great year, in fact,
had not the A's decided to call the nineteen-year-old
youngster up to the majors partway through the season.

Vida flew directly to Los Angeles, where the A's
were about to open a four-game series against the California Angels. Met at the airport by Charles O. Finley
himself, Vida was installed amid the splendor of the
first deluxe hotel he had ever slept in, then introduced
by Finley to manager Hank Bauer. The first meeting
between Blue and Finley was a strange encounter.
Finley, short, stocky, with a firm jaw and a strong
aqualine nose jutting out from below slick graying hair;
Blue, the precocious teen-ager, black, tall, looking
slightly less than his full six feet because he was built
to such even proportions. Finley, the multimillionaire;
Blue, a kid from the far side of the poverty line. Finley,
in his custom-tailored suit; Blue, whose standard dress
was a T-shirt and blue jeans. Finley, for whom everything was possible; Vida Blue, for whom only what was
necessary for survival had been possible.

And yet there was a certain rapport: perhaps owing
to Finley's outright supersalesmanship, perhaps because
he too had had to struggle for everything he'd achieved.

"My dad worked forty-seven years in the steel mills,"
he was fond of recalling. "We always lived from week

to week. The roof never leaked, but there were no frills."

The date of Vida's arrival in L.A. was July 18. At their first meeting, Bauer told Blue that he was scheduled to start the second game of the doubleheader two days hence, on July 20.

Vida was flabbergasted. The jump from Class AA Birmingham to the big leagues seemed to him like a leap into interstellar space. Los Angeles was another planet—peopled with men like Finley who wore diamond-studded cuff links, men like Bauer, who had played with the Yankees during their heyday of Mantle, Berra, Raschi, Lopat, Reynolds, and DiMaggio. His opponent on July 20, Bauer told him, would be Angel pitcher Andy Messersmith. In his second year with the Angels, Messersmith was currently 7–7, but would eventually compile a fine 16–11 record, with a 2.52 ERA.

And when Vida stepped into the Oakland dugout that day, then up the steps and onto the sidelines for his pregame warm-ups, all he could see were faces— thousands of them, more faces up in those stands than he had ever seen congregated in one spot in his entire life.

Messersmith had no trouble with the Oakland hitters that first half inning, setting the side down in order. And then it was Vida's moment to stride out to the mound, glove loosely clutched in his right hand, his long, loping strides and impassive face projecting a calm that the turbulence in his stomach belied.

And then he was out there, set on a dirt podium

raised sixteen inches above the infield, with the crowd a
tapestry of mouths emitting interminable sound. In
the outfield behind him was Reggie Jackson, with 36
homers to his credit so far that year and well ahead of
Roger Maris' record-setting pace. Turning away from
the batters' box after he'd finished his warm-up pitches,
Vida stared directly down the third-base line—and
found his gaze locked into Sal Bando's. Bando had
been selected as the American League's All-Star third
baseman.

What a change it was from playing with guys whom
no one had ever heard of, whom no one would *ever*
hear of, back in Birmingham.

And soon Vida found out that the difference between
the majors was more than one of style. Falling behind
the Angels' second batter, third baseman Aurelio Rodriguez, three balls and one strike, Vida did what he had
been doing all the way up from high school. Rearing
back, he threw his ace in the hole, a searing fast ball
low and down the middle of the plate.

But this wasn't Mansfield or Burlington or even
Birmingham. Rodriguez had been expecting it. Aurelio
leaned every ounce of his body into his swing, caught
the ball with the fat part of the bat, and blasted Blue's
pitch right out of the ball park. The next two batters
also got a piece of the ball, but their attempts were
flagged down by Oakland outfielders. And losing 1–0,
Vida didn't make a mistake for the next one and two-
thirds innings.

With two out in the bottom half of the third, Vida
faced Angel first baseman Jim Spencer, who had been

called up early in the season from the Angels' Hawaii farm club in the Pacific Coast League. In 1968 Spencer had belted 28 home runs for El Paso of the Texas League, becoming in the process the league's champ in that category. Since then, however, he'd been having trouble with curve balls at Hawaii and Los Angeles, and his power output had shrunk considerably.

But Vida Blue wasn't throwing him curves. Vida threw two fast balls by him for strikes, and when he came back with a third, Spencer timed it perfectly and drove it over the fence for another home run.

Vida avoided more mistakes until the bottom half of the sixth inning. In the interim, his teammates had scored. Going into the last half of the sixth, he was behind by only a single run, 2–1.

And then the errors of judgment came in a flurry. He gave up a walk, three hits, and three runs. Hank Bauer had seen enough. He walked out of the mound, and Blue moved quickly off for the ritual shower. Blue had been knocked out of the first major-league game he ever pitched. And in five and a third innings, he had managed only one strikeout. For a pitcher who depended heavily on a fast ball to do his work for him, the circumstance smelled of disaster.

The next time he started was back in Oakland, against the New York Yankees. Stan Bahnsen had posted a 17–12 record to win Rookie of the Year honors the previous year. (Ironically, of course, while Bahnsen had been beating the best the American League had to offer, Vida Blue had toiled that '68

season in lowly Class A, in obscurity with Burlington.)
In 1969, though, Bahnsen was suffering from what
ballplayers refer to as sophomore slump, and would
eventually wind up with a nightmarish 9–16 record
and an ERA of 3.83. If Vida could avoid making the
costly errors that he'd made against the Angels, his
teammates told him, they were sure they could give him
a cushion of runs to work with.

And they were as good as their word. In the home
half of the first inning, Reggie Jackson homered, Sal
Bando doubled, and Danny Cater drove Bando home
for the A's second run with a sharp single to left field.
Vida held the Yankees scoreless until the sixth inning,
with the A's adding another run in the interim to make
his lead 3–0. But from the sixth inning on, Vida found
trouble at every turn. By the bottom half of the eighth
his 3–0 lead had become a 3–4 Yankee lead. His teammates, not his pitching, saved the game for him, when
the A's hitters came up with two runs in the bottom of
the eighth. Even then, Vida gave up a run in the ninth
and barely managed to preserve a 6–5 victory.

Seven hits, three walks, and four runs in nine innings.
He had won his first major-league victory, but the men
who knew credited the win more to the Oakland bats
than to Blue's arm.

Against the Boston Red Sox on August 3, Vida
couldn't retire a single batter in the fifth inning. Before
Oakland manager Hank Bauer lifted him for a reliever,
he'd given up a total of five runs. The A's again managed to come back and win, but no credit to Vida. He
started again five days later, with the Yankees for oppo-

nents. This time Vida managed to last seven and a half innings, giving up eight hits and four walks. When Vida left, the A's were losing 2–1, but again a combination of clutch late-inning Oakland batting, plus effective relief pitching, preserved his record at 1–1.

He didn't start again that season.

In retrospect, his trip to Oakland seemed like a mistake. The A's had brought him along too fast. In 12 appearances with the A's in '69, he pitched 42 innings, winning 1 game, losing another, giving up 34 runs and 18 walks.

Still, his record seemed like a respectable debut, given his youth and lack of experience. But in fact, it was a near disaster. Although his fast ball hummed frequently enough to strike out 24 batters, the fast ball was all he had. And major-league batters can hit a fast ball pitcher—when that single pitch is a pitcher's repertoire—from here to kingdom come. Which they did.

Says Blue himself: "I couldn't control my breaking stuff then. Everybody knew it, and all a guy had to do was sit back and wait for the fast ball."

Al Kaline, star of the Detroit Tigers, had done exactly that. The first game he faced Blue—a no-decision encounter for Vida—superstar Kaline had hit 3 towering home runs in a row. Overall, 10 more home runs in those 42 innings brought Blue's giveaway total to 13 for his major-league debut. In comparison, during his 14 starts for Birmingham that same year, Blue had surrendered but 1 home run in his first 95 2/3 innings. Just how poorly in fact he performed is illustrated by his atrocious 6.21 earned run average.

He was still a fast ball pitcher in search of a curve. But unlike Birmingham and Burlington before it, even the best fast ball in the world was only good for a return ticket from the majors to the minors. The A's had erred was the consensus. And in erring, perhaps, they had possibly ruined the best prospect they'd ever had.

But Finley had invested in more than a pitcher. He had invested in a personality—a character indomitable enough to withstand the temptations of college recruiters, responsible enough to place the welfare of his family over his own immediate interest. Blue had come a long way in a short time. He was not going to let a minor defeat shatter his confidence in himself.

In answer to those who said the A's had made a mistake in bringing him up to the big leagues in 1969, Vida later replied: "No, they didn't bring me up too soon. I think I was capable of pitching in the majors even then, but I was at a disadvantage by not knowing the other players and their capabilities and preferences. But it was good experience. I learned a lot. When I returned, I was a lot better prepared."

Instead of being shattered by his premature exposure to the likes of Kaline, Yastrzemski and Co., his initial failure only made Blue more determined to succeed the next chance he got. For a nineteen-year-old, he showed uncommon fortitude. He didn't have a curve ball, but he had guts.

4

Capturing Control

At the tail end of that 1969 season Vida was called to serve six months active duty with his Army Reserve unit. He had lots of free time at camp and spent much of it—as his drastic experience of major-league fast ball hitters demanded—working on his change-up and curve, realizing as never before that without these additions to his pitching arsenal he would never stick in the big leagues.

Because of his military service, Vida arrived late at the A's training camp in Mesa, Arizona, before the 1970 season. The A's had already departed, en route to their opening game of the season in Kansas City, against the Royals. Likewise, the Iowa Oaks and Birmingham A's were traveling to their opening games, too—leaving only the Burlington Bees in camp when Vida arrived. His immediate reaction was a measure

48

of how badly he rated his big-league performance the previous year and how badly shaken was his self-confidence: "Oh, m'God, they're shipping me back to Burlington and Class A ball!" So, before he had even unpacked his bags, a terrified Vida Blue was calling scouting director Phil Seghi long distance to find out where he'd been assigned.

Seghi could barely restrain his laughter, but managed to keep his voice straight and inform Vida that Finley and Co. were still deciding whether Vida would go back to Birmingham for another year of Double A or whether he'd be sent up to the Iowa Oaks, Class Triple A. At no time, he reassured Vida, had anyone ever considered sending him back to lowly Burlington.

In retrospect, with one of those ironic twists of fate that spice every man's life, Vida's late arrival at training camp was to have an enduring effect on his future career. For had he not arrived late, he would never have met the man with whose help he finally learned to control his curve and change-up. Thirty-three-year-old Juan Pizarro also arrived late to camp. Pizarro had been pitching winter ball in Hawaii and was ordered to spend a few weeks at Mesa before he joined the parent club in Oakland.

Juan Pizarro was a journeyman left-hander who'd been playing professional ball since 1956, when he broke in with Jacksonville of the Sally League. Having had his ups and downs over the next five years, he finally made it to the big leagues on a permanent basis in 1959, when he joined the Milwaukee Braves. In 1961 he was traded across league frontiers to the Chicago White Sox, with which he was to have his best years. In 1964 he was 19–9 but was never again so effective. From Chicago, in 1967 he went back to the National League, with Pittsburgh. In 1968 he crossed lines again to pitch for Boston. During the '69 season he was traded to Cleveland, which then dealt him to the Oakland Athletics.

Pizarro was entering his fifteenth year of professional ball, having spent eleven of them in the major leagues. Like Vida, he'd entered pro ball at the age of nineteen. Like Vida, he'd known poverty, for which professional baseball was the only viable escape route. Pizarro had also carved out his best years with the use of a single tool—a blazing fast ball. Now, however, with his stamina eroded by age, he had developed a variety of sharp breaking "junk" pitches, saving his fast ball to break the batter's timing and to set him up for wide-angling curves.

Early on in camp Juan was attracted to the cocky kid from Mansfield with the slingshot arm. Blue, on the other hand, was too much a novice and too much an extrovert to be intimidated by the usual self-segregation practiced by continental and Caribbean blacks. He had learned that whatever success he had had before, major-league ball was a coat of another color. So, as their friendship developed in easy, laconic stages, Blue determined to be as receptive as possible to Pizarro's criticisms—based on fifteen years' experience.

"You gotta have somethin' else beside the fast one," Pizarro told him. And then the veteran left-hander proceeded to show his twenty-year-old protégé how to throw the breaking ball. He also taught him how to pace himself, how to mix his pitches.

The progress Vida made in those first few weeks convinced management that if Blue still needed seasoning before being thrown to the American League wolves, he *was* ready for baseball one cut below the majors. Vida was told to report to the Iowa Oaks, a Triple A club based in Des Moines.

In his short stay with the A's that previous season Vida had had a chance for the first time to see how major-league ballplayers lived—in luxury hotels, with fans clamoring for their autographs, shopowners willing to provide them with goods—free for the mere fact of their patronage. Triple A was still a step below major-league affluence, but it was a far cry from the sleazy hotels of Class A Burlington, the measly meal allowance offered in Class AA Birmingham. At Des Moines, the team traveled by "motor coach" rather than "bus." They stayed in first-class hotels. No color TV in every room like the deluxe establishments, but black and white to while away those interminable hours between the ninth inning of one game and the opening pitch of the next.

Getting that late start in spring training, Vida didn't pitch for the Oaks until the club was three weeks into its schedule. But his first start—on April 29, against the Oklahoma City 89ers—was, from the point of view of Charlie Finley's investment two years before, well worth waiting for. Vida beat the 89ers 7–1, setting en route a new club record for strikeouts in a single game. The only hitter who really got a piece of a Vida Blue pitch was, appropriately, Cesar Cedeno, now in the outfield of the Houston Astros and a young player whom many have tabbed as a future superstar. But even Cedeno's seventh-inning home run couldn't spoil Blue's exciting debut.

And from that first performance on, Vida got even better. On May 6, he shut out the Tulsa Oilers, 4–0. On May 16, Vida beat the Evansville Triplets for his third victory in as many starts. Proof of exactly how effective his new change-up and curve were making his fast ball, in three games he had struck out an amazing total of 40 batters. After barely winning his fourth start, he beat the Omaha Royals, 2–1, with 11 strikeouts, to make a total of 54 in five games. On May 26, Vida's sixth start resulted in a sixth straight victory, as the Indianapolis Indians went down before his fast ball, 7–2.

So, in that 1970 season, Blue had put Pizarro's teachings to immediate and effective use. Appearing in 17 games, he pitched 133 innings, winning 12 while losing only 3 games. Gaining more confidence in his ability to set up batters for his fast ball with sly breaking stuff, Blue found he was able to capture that heretofore-missing ingredient—control. He walked only 55 batters, while leading the league in strikeouts with 165. He gave up only 32 earned runs all season to finish with an ERA of 2.17.

"After the first month of the season," Vida recalled later, "I was something like 4–0, and I figured I was ready to come up. I didn't need more than one and a half months down in Des Moines."

The A's agreed, and when Oakland reliever Johnny Roland went on the twenty-one-day disabled list with an injury, Blue was called up to the parent club and sent to sit out in the bullpen. But he was there merely as a roster-filling warm body. No one thought to use him during the eleven days he was up with the A's, and he was sent back to Iowa without having thrown one pitch in a game situation.

Vida was so disgusted he nearly jumped the club and went home. But reason—and the staunch counsel of his mother back in Mansfield—prevailed, and he returned to Des Moines. Ironically enough, in retrospect it seems that taking him away from the Oaks—yet refusing to pitch him with the A's—was another costly error on the part of Oakland management.

For the Oaks finished second in the American Association, only one game out—presumably a game Blue would have won if he hadn't been torn away from the club for eleven days. On the other hand, over the final month of the season the A's fell farther behind the Minnesota Twins, finishing nine games out of first place in their division. Undoubtedly, Blue could have shrunk that margin, too.

In any case, by the end of August Vida was back wearing the uniform of the Iowa Oaks. Even though he'd been ignored in his short stay with the parent club, that was a cut above the disaster that he'd suffered his first time up with Oakland. So he tightened his belt, toughened up his mental attitude to squeeze the resentment from memory, and went back to work. On August 27 he beat the Evansville Triplets again, this time giving up only two hits in a 5–0 win. In his second start after returning to Des Moines, he won again. He lost his last start, but nothing—not even his senseless trip to Oakland—could spoil this season of triumph for him.

And all frustrations and disappointments faded in the flush of excitement when—with the annual swelling of the rosters to forty—Vida was once again called up, on September 1, to the parent club. Although the world of sports was blithely oblivious to the fact, the stage was set for the debut of the most exciting baseball rookie the game had ever seen.

"The first time I came up," says Vida, "it was like going into enemy grounds without knowing where the minefields were located. But when I came back, I knew where to put my feet down with sufficient caution to avoid the mines."

Blue was accompanied on this trip by a group of teammates from Des Moines, and all of them were lodged at the Edgewater Hotel near the Oakland Coliseum. After a few days of adjusting to their luxurious surroundings, the A's—and Vida Blue—were airborne toward the Windy City. And Vida Blue was designated the starting pitcher for the opening game of the series against the Chicago White Sox on September 6.

When Vida strolled out to the mound in the second half of the first inning, he had a one-run cushion to work with. It would be a test for him, this first game. Pitchers who are greeted—as Vida had been the previous season—by a barrage of home runs, who fail dramatically in their major-league baptisms—sometimes never recover. Their confidence destroyed irreparably, they are tabbed for the rest of their careers as good minor-leaguers, who had everything necessary to compete successfully in the big leagues—except courage. The minors are full of them—hitters who regularly crack the .300 mark, hurlers who are good for 16 to 20 games every minor-league season they pitch. They, like Vida's friend with the Burlington Bees, Stan Jones, become the career minor-leaguers, caught irretrievably on landings between escalators while their teammates are on their way up or the way down.

Vida's antagonist for Chicago that day was Joel Horlen. Twenty-six that year, the six-foot, 170-pound native Californian had signed with the White Sox in 1959 as a $50,000-bonus baby. He'd joined the White Sox in 1961 and was now in his ninth year as a major-leaguer. His best year had been 1967, when he had compiled a 19-6 record, with a 2.06 ERA that was best in the entire league. He had also pitched a no-hitter against Detroit on September 10 that year.

His problem throughout his career had been control. In 1966 he had led the American League in wild pitches, with 14. In 1968, the year after his super-season, he hit 14 batsman to lead the league. Now, at thirty-three he had pretty much solved his control problems, but too late. Becoming "cute," he would manage to hang on for a few more years, but in 1970 he was on his way to his worst season ever, finishing up finally with a 6-16 won/lost record—and a disastrous 4.87 ERA.

Perhaps with more pressure riding on his shoulders

than ever before, Vida bore down that first half inning as if he were pitching for his life. He set the White Sox down in order. Vida gave up a run in the second inning but then set the White Sox down in order again in the third.

After the third inning, the score was 3–1, Oakland. Horlen had been lifted in the second inning, and the Chicago pitcher was Jerry Crider. With two Oakland runners on base, Vida came up to bat in the fourth inning. His first time up Horlen had struck him out. This time Crider got the count to 3-2, then tried to blaze a fast ball by Vida for the third strike. Instead, Vida hit it squarely and watched in amazement as the ball sailed out of the ball park, making the score 6–2, Oakland.

However, so elated was he over his feat with the bat that he neglected his pitching. After he gave up three runs in his fifth inning, he was taken out of the game for reliever Rollie Fingers. The A's eventually won, 7–4, and Vida had been the batting star. But he was being paid to pitch, not to hit—and Rollie Fingers had earned credit for the victory.

In total, in 4 1/3 innings, Vida had allowed 4 runs on 7 hits, striking out 4 and giving up 2 walks. It wasn't a performance to rave about, despite his home run. After all, he wasn't going to stick in the majors on the strength of his power hitting.

His second start was an improvement. He beat the Kansas City Royals, 3–0, on a one-hitter—a single to Pat Riley with two out in the eighth inning. His performance startled the baseball world, drowsing off at the end of a 162-game schedule, with the pennants all but decided.

His third start was against the Milwaukee Brewers. Vida was off again, lasting only five and a third innings when he left the game with the score tied, 3–3. Bob Locker relieved him and was credited with the victory when Oakland pulled out a 5–3 win.

When the A's returned to Oakland, Vida left the Edgewater Hotel and rented a room in a boardinghouse used by the club periodically to house players. It was a significant step. Despite his inability to finish two of the three games he had started, his 3–0 one-hit victory over the Royals had convinced him that he could pitch well enough to risk putting down a deposit on a room for the two weeks left in the season.

His next start was against the Minnesota Twins. Killebrew, Tovar, Carew, Oliva, and Co. had only to beat the A's in order to clinch the Western Division title. On paper it seemed an easy task.

Pitching against the Twins' Jim Perry, who was completing a 24-12 season as the top winner in the American League, Vida set down the first three batters he faced, two on strikeouts. And in the bottom half of that first inning, the A's got to Jim Perry. Lead-off hitter Campy Campaneris started the inning off with a sharp triple to left field. Joe Rudi walked. The A's third batter, right-fielder Felipe Alou, took two strikes before hitting a low liner right at Rod Carew, who forced Rudi out at second base, then threw to first to nip Alou by a step, completing the double play. But with heads-up baserunning, in the interim Campaneris had crossed the plate with the A's first run of the afternoon.

The score remained 1–0, Oakland, for the next five innings. More important, while Perry gave up five hits, Vida Blue gave up none.

And in the bottom half of the eighth inning Campaneris got to Perry again, blasting the ball right out of the park with two teammates riding home in front of him, to make the score 4–0. Perry got tagged for two more runs that inning, to make the score 6–0.

And Vida Blue was still pitching a no-hitter.

By now of course, he realized that he was on the verge of something spectacular. For the first six innings he had been so intent on simply getting batter after batter out that he'd been unaware he was pitching a perfect game. Nor had any of his teammates reminded him. They were obeying an unwritten rule—a superstition ballplayers have that to talk about pitching a no-hitter before the feat is accomplished is the surest way to prevent the perfect game.

But at the start of the ninth inning, with the A's leading 6–0 and Vida three outs away from immortality, he *knew* all right! He was sweating, and not from heat. His throat was like sandpaper. The palms of his hands were clammy.

"I just kept thinking," Vida recalled after the game, "no-hitter, no-hitter. It just went through my mind, over and over and over."

He bore down—fast ball, curve, change-up, fast ball, curve, fast ball, change-up—a dizzying blend of off-speed, on-speed, but on-target pitches that sent the first two Minnesota batters reeling back to the dugout, strikeout victims. Then, with two outs—one out away from a perfect game—Vida faced one of the toughest hitters in baseball, one of the greatest competitors the game has known.

Thirty-year-old Cesar Tovar, a native of the teeming slums of Caracas, Venezuela, was in his fifth full season with the Twins. Besides his competitiveness and durability (he was known as the Iron Man), Tovar's versatility was a legend. In a game with the Twins in 1968, for example, he had played every one of the nine positions, including pitcher. (In his one inning on the mound, he had struck out one batter and walked another, giving up no hits and no runs.) When Vida faced him, he was having his best year in the majors at bat and would eventually finish with a .300 average. His speed and daring on the bases would gain him over the season the highest total of triples (13) in the league, and the second-best doubles total (36). With a 6–0 lead, better to face home run champ Killebrew, who would strike out as often as he hit the fences. In a situation where there was a no-hitter on the line, there was probably no more tenacious opponent in the American League than the versatile Venezuelan. Tovar wouldn't quit.

Would Vida?

Tovar took the first pitch—a called strike. Vida reared back, kicking high off the mound, and delivered a deceptive curve. Low, ball one. With a sudden hush sealing the lips of the nearly 5,000 fans in the stadium, Blue started into his motion—then Tovar stepped out of the box. He bent down, picked up dirt, and rubbed it into his hands. Giving his cap a final tug, he stepped back into the batter's box, shifted the bat high above his shoulder, and waited. He knew Blue would throw the fast ball.

Vida did, high and inside. Tovar struck at it but connected just inches above his wrists. Oakland catcher Gene Tenace threw off his mask, charging down the first-base line toward the dugout with his eyes glued to the towering foul pop. *Waiting, waiting*—to the 5,000 fans, to Vida Blue, to catcher Tenace, it seemed an eternity before the ball completed its descent and landed *crack* in the belly pocket of the catcher's mitt.

Jubilation, vindication! Vida Blue had entered the record books. It was September 21, 1970, and Vida Blue had stunned the sports world by pitching a no-hit, no-run, 6–0 victory. The only slip from perfection was a fourth-inning walk to Harmon Killebrew.

Said a jubilant Blue after the game: "I threw Killebrew a curve on a 3–1 pitch. We were trying to keep the ball away from him, because the score was still 1–0. He can hit out of the ball park."

But in two other appearances, Blue had struck out the American League home run champ, and after the game the tough Minnesota slugger said, "He had exceptional stuff. He got me with fast balls—and I mean *fast* balls!" Using the breaking pitch sparingly but to great effect (20 of his 114 pitches were curve balls), Blue had allowed only four balls to be hit as far as the outfield, and his infielders had to contend with only two moderately difficult fielding chances throughout the entire game.

After the game reporters were notified that Vida was one of the least ecstatic players in the clubhouse. So someone asked him if he was excited.

"A thing like this," he replied calmly, "is bound to shake up the best of them."

And then he phoned his mother.

Afterward Charlie Finley called Vida from Chicago, informing him that he had earned a $2,000 bonus. Catcher Gene Tenace received $1,000.

"He gives little awards like that for no-hitters, pinch-hit home runs, and other such feats," Vida said. "I hope to get more phone calls like that."

The second bonus Vida received that day was the bottle of champagne Twins' manager Bill Rigney had been chilling for the postgame pennant-winning celebration that he and almost everyone had anticipated— except twenty-year-old Vida Blue.

5

Star or Comet?

Vida pitched in two more games that season but wasn't involved in the decision in either one. Overall, his final record with Oakland was 2-0. Pitching 39 innings in 6 games, he had given up 20 hits but only 12 walks, while striking out 35 batters. His earned run average was a miserly 2.08.

The day after the season closed, confirming the A's second-place finish, owner Charlie Finley called a press conference. Manager John McNamara (who had replaced Hank Bauer at the beginning of the season) had done well, but to Finley's taste not well enough. Charlie O. wasn't investing millions only to produce a runner-up. He felt the club needed stronger leadership. Hiring and firing his tenth manager in as many years, Finley announced that in 1971 the club would be led by Dick Williams.

Williams had been in baseball since 1947, one of a long line of mediocre players who hang on in the game long after the superstars are out selling insurance. Finishing his career as a substitute infielder with the Boston Red Sox in 1960, he managed the Red Sox's Toronto farm team until he was called up to lead the parent team itself in 1967. He had arrived at a time when the Red Sox were suffering from disorganization and dissension. The year before, 1966, they'd finished a poor sixth in their division. By driving the team like a Simon Legree-in-spikes, Williams converted that sixth-place team to a pennant winner in 1967 and was named the American League's Manager of the Year.

The Red Sox didn't repeat the next season. With players accustomed to the soft permissiveness of owner Tom Yawkey (legendary for paying the league's highest salaries while tolerating the most petulant behavior from his employees), Williams began a series of feuds, in particular with superstar Carl Yastrzemski.

In one famous diatribe against Williams, a player said: "He calls you garbage, then expects you to go out and prove you aren't."

The conflict finally came to a head in 1970, and rather than reprimand some of his highly paid ball-playing prima donnas, Red Sox owner Yawkey took the easy way out and fired the manager, even though Williams' managerial *ability* was undisputed.

One man's poison is another man's meat. Unlike the Red Sox, the Athletics had no "problem children." Reggie Jackson was the nearest thing the A's had to a superstar, but even he commanded nowhere the press

—or the money—that, for example, Carl Yastrzemski did. On the other hand, Williams was reputed to be a brilliant tactician, and that appealed to the Oakland ballplayers, who were dog-tired of finishing second every year. Furthermore, everyone on the club believed that Williams would allow no interference from anyone in management; if necessary, he would go so far as to bar Finley himself from the clubhouse.

And while McNamara had been universally liked, there were those among the A's who felt that he had been too submissive to Finley, that at times Finley had been making the day-to-day managerial decisions, and that Charlie's baseball acumen was less acute than his eye for finances.

Vida and the rest of the A's adopted a wait-and-see attitude toward Williams.

In the spring of 1971, Vida Blue was a curiosity when he reported to camp at Mesa, Arizona, along with the rest of the A's pitching staff. Teammates re-called the tail end of the 1970 season and asked each other only one question. Was this guy for real? Was he an authentic star rising on the baseball horizon, or merely a comet who'd burn out on contact with the tough, day-in, day-out grind of a 162-game schedule, facing the best ballplayers in the world.

As is customary, the A's catchers and pitchers had reported to spring training camp before the rest of their teammates. That first day of spring training, Vida and his mates strolled—with some trepidation, some curi-

osity—out to center field for their formal introduction
to manager Williams.

Williams turned out to be a pleasant surprise. He
had a sense of humor; he talked in a low-keyed voice.
He was, he said, available for anyone who wanted to
talk to him about any problem at any time. There would
be no startling changes from last year's lineup. The
only change he planned to make in spring training was
one to warm the heart of any ballplayer. Unlike most
of his major-league peers, Williams was unconvinced
of the value of calisthenics as preparation for the game
of baseball. They result, he said, in more *pulled* muscles
than *loose* muscles. Laps around the field, time trials
down the first-base line—the whole range of endurance
runs and wind sprints which ballplayers usually submit
to in spring training were also to be dispensed with.

"The way to get in shape for playing baseball," said
Williams, "is to play baseball. And that's what we're
gonna do—intrasquad games, five against five—we're
gonna have some *fun!*"

After practice session that morning, while the ballplayers were soaking the Arizona sun out of their
sweat-drenched bodies, Dick Williams took time out to
explain how he could afford to alter his personality to
suit his managing needs at Oakland.

"I had to be extra tough with the Red Sox," he told
a group of reporters. "The Red Sox had finished ninth
the year before I came. They had an 'I don't give a
damn attitude,' and I had to change it to a winning
attitude. Oakland is a contender," he added. "They've

finished a strong second for two years running. Basically, what I have to do here is have the A's eliminate mistakes, mental errors, play good sound fundamental baseball and win head to head against the Minnesota Twins."

How did his pitching stack up for the coming campaign?

"I've got a hell of a pitching staff here," Williams enthused. "They're one hundred percent better than the pitching staff I had in Boston. Right now I can't count on Odom, but that still leaves me with Hunter and Blue. Anything Odom can give me will just be a plus."

Johnny Lee "Blue Moon" Odom had been with the Oakland ball club since the '68 season, compiling a fine 16-10 record during his rookie year. The next season, 1969, he was 15-6, but in 1970 he had slipped to a 9-8 record, with a poor earned run average of 3.81. In fact, postseason X rays showed that he had been pitching with a floating bone chip in his right elbow. The past winter he had been dispatched to the Mayo Clinic for surgery. He eventually reported to spring training one day late but was prohibited by his doctors from pitching for an entire month. Thus, when the team eventually moved on to Oakland, Odom was left behind at Mesa to recuperate at his own speed.

Chuck Dobson, whom Williams was counting on as one of his three starters, was a twenty-six-year-old right-hander who had joined the A's in 1966, when the A's were in Kansas City. A six-foot-four-inch, 200-pound fast ball pitcher with loads of potential, Dobson had yet to live up to it. Up to now he had been a .500

pitcher, compiling a 10-10 record in 1967, 12-14 in 1968, 15-13 in '69, and 16-15 in 1970. Only one season in his professional career had he ever averaged fewer than 3.00 earned runs per game—and that was back in 1965, with Lewiston of the Northwest League. In six seasons with the A's, his overall ERA was 3.53! So despite manager Williams' faith in him, Dobson's ability to carry his share of a three-man rotation was suspect.

The A's third starter (besides Blue and Dobson), Jim "Catfish" Hunter, had joined the parent club at the age of nineteen, 1965, never having pitched organized minor-league ball. (In 1964 he'd been with Daytona Beach of the Florida State League but had been on the disabled list for the entire season.) In his first season he was 8-8. In 1968 he was 13-13. In 1966, 1967, and 1969 he had lost more games than he had won.

Then, in 1970, he had metamorphosed from an erratic but promising kid into an 18-game winner. Like Dobson, however, he still managed to lose (14 games) almost as many as he won. And his 3.81 ERA suggested that he was lucky not to end up with a record of 14-18. Again, a pitcher with promise, but not—at that point—the kind you'd wager your money on in consecutive outings.

When Odom came back to full health, he would be the fourth starter. Collectively, Dobson, Hunter and Odom had, in 1970, won 43 games while losing 37. Overall, their aggregate earned run average was 3.79. And this was the staff that Williams argued was better than his Red Sox starters? Not on your life—unless,

of course, he was already counting heavily on Vida
Blue.

Until Odom recovered fully and was able to take his
place in the rotation, Williams decided to start Diego
Segui, the A's top reliever. Rollie Fingers would share
relief work with Segui and would also be available as a
spot starter.

After a promising exhibition season, Blue was tapped
by manager Dick Williams to pitch the season's opener
against the Washington Senators in the nation's capital.

"I think we were all a little nervous," Blue said later.
"Not because it was Washington and the President
might be there, but just because it was the opening day
of the season."

President Nixon wasn't there for that opener. With
Vice President Agnew also away on business of state,
Nixon blended his version of sports and patriotism and
came up with Master Sergeant Daniel Pitzer (a Vietnam veteran who'd spent four years in a Vietcong
prison compound) as his relief hurler.

But the pitcher of prime concern to Vida Blue and
the rest of the A's was the Senators' Dick Bosman. The
twenty-six-year-old Bosman had topped the league in
ERA in 1969 (2.19) while compiling a record of 14-5.
In 1970, he had won 16 while losing 12—quite a feat
with the weak hitting and error-prone Senators.

In the top of the first inning, the A's went down in
order. But after Vida struck out the Senators' lead-off
hitter, rookie shortstop Toby Harrah singled to center
field. The next batter popped out to Sal Bando at third
base. Then Mike Epstein (who would later that season

play so important a role for the A's in their pennant-winning drive) singled to left, driving Harrah all the way to third. Harrah and Epstein both scored on Senator catcher Paul Casanova's line single into right field. And by the end of the inning the Senators were leading, 4–0.

Vida didn't pitch another full inning that day. In the second, losing his composure completely, the young left-hander gave up four walks to force in a run. A passed ball, which could have been called a wild pitch, allowed another run to score, and Williams came out to the mound. Vida was lifted, but his successors fared just as poorly, as Washington won, 8–0.

No one in Washington dreamed that the pitcher they saw defeated that day would six months later be Richard Nixon's guest at the White House.

After this disappointing beginning, Vida went on to reel off 10 straight victories. In his second start, against the Royals, whom he'd one-hitted the previous September, he struck out 13, to pitch a 3-hit, 5–0 victory in a game shortened by rain to six innings. Next the Milwaukee Brewers fell to Blue, 2–0, with Vida giving up only 2 hits, both of them feeble singles.

The Brewer game was an important victory for the A's. Up to that date the club had lost 4 of its first 6 games. And just what effect losing could have on Dick Williams' mild-mannered approach to managing was illustrated by an incident reporters witnessed on the A's arrival in Milwaukee. The ballplayers had already boarded the charter bus that would shuttle them to their downtown hotel, when a member of the airline flight

crew ran breathlessly up to the bus and told Williams
that a battery-powered megaphone was missing.

Now, for the first time, the A's saw the manager who
had earned the reputation of a drill sergeant at Boston.
Angrily leaping up from his seat at the front of the bus,
Williams called the team to attention. Using the missing megaphone as an example of the kind of mental
and emotional immaturity that leads to a losing attitude, Williams proceeded to ennumerate in painful
detail the mental lapses, bonehead plays, and "I don't
give a damn" attitude that had caused the A's 4 defeats
in 6 games. According to reporters on the scene, Williams told his team:

"Some of you think you can be awful, but I can be
worse than any of you. I've been mild up to now.
There will be no booze served on our airplanes this
trip. I suggest that you stay in your rooms the entire
trip. And if any of you want to telephone Charlie,"
he added, with undisguised sarcasm, "I have three
numbers where he can be reached."

This last barb was, of course, a reference to the fact
that dissatisfied players had gone over John Mc-
Namara's head to owner Finley. And Finley, it was
rumored, had not hesitated to countermand Mc-
Namara's orders, if he thought one of his pet players
had been slighted.

When Williams completed his diatribe, he sat down
facing front. Only when the megaphone had been returned to the waiting crew member did he give the
order to move.

Besides restoring the megaphone to its rightful

owners, Williams' show of strength seemed to have had a long-range effect: The A's, beginning with Vida's victory over the Brewers, won 12 of their next 13 games.

The White Sox were Vida's third successive victims. They managed six hits and two runs, but Blue struck out 11, coasting home to victory on an 11-run cushion.

In his fourth straight victory—against the California Angels—Vida gave up three runs and his first home run of the season (to Jim Spencer), but beat the Angels, 7–3, on five hits.

He was equally stingy in his first encounter with the world champion Baltimore Orioles on April 26, giving up only five singles and striking out nine batters as he defeated them, while pitching under pressure, 1–0.

For his sixth victory, he beat the Cleveland Indians, 3–1, on six hits.

"Vida just gets better as he goes along," said manager Dick Williams in the clubhouse after the game. "My only worry about him is that he stay healthy."

In his eighth start of the season, Vida faced the Detroit Tigers, who, in his premature trip to the majors in 1969, had blasted him all the way from Oakland, California, to Des Moines, Iowa. This time they faced a new Vida Blue—a matured twenty-year-old who could direct his blazing fast ball with the accuracy of a heat-seeking missile, who was periodically able to slip in a sudden breaking curve to upset a batter's timing, who had the skills to win and the guts not to quit.

Two years before, superstar Al Kaline, powerful Willie Horton, All-Star catcher Bill Freehan, and All-

Star second baseman Dick McAuliffe had broken
Vida's confidence. With a vengeance born of the pride
that was to become his trademark, Vida bore down on
each of them—and struck each of them out *twice*.
Like a fighter who gives that something extra to wipe
out an opponent who had stained his record with defeat early in his career, Vida pitched with a vengeance,
giving up only four hits—all singles—to beat his
nemesis, 5–0.

After that game, Kaline told the press how much he
was impressed with the new Blue.

"He's more of a pitcher now," said the great Tiger
right fielder. "I always remember him throwing hard,
but he's got an awful lot more confidence. He's more
relaxed out there now. That helps a lot. He throws as
good as anyone in the league. What really impressed
me," Kaline added, "was that when he got in a jam,
he could strike somebody out. That's very important."

But Vida was careful not to let the accolades go to
his head. "I'm telling myself, 'Don't get cocky. Give
your services to the press and media, be nice to the
kids, throw a baseball into the stands once in a while.'
I've got to be modest about the whole thing," he added.
"You'll never hear me brag about what I've done."

"He just gets better as he goes along," said manager
Dick Williams, doing the bragging for Vida. "I'd like to
keep him in a glass case between starts. We don't have
any worries about him. He's a nice kid. But you can't
really call him a kid. He's, well, he's a man."

In his ninth start, Vida beat Baltimore's ace right-
hander, Jim Palmer, for his second straight victory over

the Orioles. Vida pitched a four-hitter, winning 2–1. The fact that the Birds had managed to scratch across a run prompted the lumbering Boog Powell to exclaim after the game: "We got nothing the first time against him. We got one this time. The way we're improving," he added with tongue in cheek, "we might get two runs the next time."

Other Orioles were even more explicit in their praise. Said manager Earl Weaver after that second consecutive defeat by Blue: "If we could have looked for his fast ball walking off the bench, we'd have been all right. But he kept getting that curve over and we didn't know what to expect."

Frank Robinson was even more impressed. "That's the best stuff I've seen in a long, long time," he said.

"Vida has three things going for him," explained Oakland catcher Dave Duncan. "First, he's overpowering. Second, his ball moves. Third, he's sneaky. He has that nice, easy motion, so you think you can hit him. But you can't pick up the ball until it's too late."

In his next outing, against the Royals again, Blue almost lost one. But the A's rallied to get him off the hook and preserve his unbeaten streak.

Then he beat the Brewers on three hits, 3–0, for his ninth victory.

In his eleventh start of the season, Vida faced another Oakland hex, Jim Perry. Before Blue had beaten him with his no-hitter the previous September, Perry had defeated Oakland eleven straight times since August 7, 1966. Now Vida made it two straight victories over Perry, beating the Twins, 3–1, and giving up only five singles to win his tenth consecutive victory.

The next time out he lost to the Red Sox.

Then he beat Denny McLain of the Senators, who had held nine straight wins over the A's dating back to September 7, 1966.

So by the end of May Vida was the hottest pitcher in baseball, with an 11-2 record. He had struck out 69 men in 62 innings. He had pitched 7 consecutive complete games, 4 shutouts in a row. He had a two-hitter, a three-hitter, 2 four-hitters, a five-hitter, and 2 six-hitters.

6

What Good Is a Cadillac?

On June 2 the Yankees arranged the promotion that was becoming standard fare every time Vida Blue arrived at a major-league city. Calling the game Blue was slated to pitch Blue Tuesday, Yankee management permitted anyone who could authenticate his surname as "Blue" to get into the ball park free. Vida did all his 3,000 namesakes proud, too, easily beating the Yanks for victory No. 12. By now he was one of the sensations of this and any season.

On June 12 he faced the Yankees for the second time in a month and beat them, 13–3, for win No. 13. Four days later he defeated the Washington Senators, 3–1, to avenge his opening-day loss. Next, on the twenty-first of that fabulous month, Vida took on the powerful Minnesota Twins, eking out a tight victory by a 3–2 margin, for win No. 15.

His next scheduled outing was for Friday, June 25. As a special treat Charlie Finley flew Vida's mother, brother, and four sisters up from Mansfield for the game. It was the first time any of them had seen Vida pitch professionally. And he rewarded them by pitching a 7–0 shutout against the Kansas City Royals.

Of course, the reason Finley had gone to the expense of bringing the Blue family to Oakland was that the following day, Saturday, was Vida Day in Oakland. For openers, with Finley on hand beside a microphone set up on the playing field, Sallie Blue was escorted out to thunderous applause. Moments later the center field gates opened, and a 1971 Cadillac Eldorado charged onto the field like an elegant metallic bull. The Motor Vehicle Registrar of the State of California had been conveniently planted at Finley's shoulder. With Blue standing beside his mother, registrar McLaughlin handed Vida a certificate of ownership and a set of plates, bearing the inscription "V-Blue." Finley then made a formal presentation, and Vida a brief acceptance speech. The $10,000 car was, of course, later to become a bitter bone of contention between them— Finley using it as an example of his generosity beyond the call of duty and Blue passing the gift off lightly as a publicity gimmick.

In his next outing, against Minnesota, the Twins finally broke Vida's string of victories against them, handing him his third defeat. However, on the fourth of July he came back to win his seventeenth game of the season against the California Angels by a score of 5–3.

Vida was so overpowering in the first half of the season that at times batters weren't sure what he was throwing. He came out of a high kick and his fast ball seemed to take off as it neared the plate. But all hands agreed he was some kind of pitcher.

"He's quite a guy," said manager Ralph Houk of the Yankees. "His curve ball sets the hitters up for the fast ball. And the fast ball really moves. He's really some athlete."

"Vida is a good solid young man," said Oakland manager Dick Williams. "And something that seems to get overlooked is that he's good for baseball. Look how the crowds turn out when he's listed to pitch."

More than 1,000,000 fans would spin the turnstiles on days when Vida pitched that season, and there is little doubt that he saved the Oakland home gate from disaster. For the full season, the A's would average 22,000 fans on days when Vida pitched, and 12,000 when he didn't.

By the All-Star game Vida was 17-3, with 17 complete games and 188 strikeouts in 184 innings. More telling even than his phenomenal record was his heretofore-unheard-of 1.42 earned run average.

With statistics like these throughout the first half of the season bookmakers had been making Blue a prohibitive favorite, up to 3–1, almost every time he pitched. And there was no doubt that Vida was making the most of his celebrity status. "I'm single . . . make sure you mention that," he told a reporter, grinning. "I don't smoke, and I take only an occasional drink. In Oakland I share an apartment with Tommy

Davis, and I call my mother on the phone at least once a week," he added, dictating the kind of image he wanted to promote.

And he was just as much an attraction on the road as at home. Wherever he went he added thousands of dollars to the coffers of the home team. One incident, as early in the season as July 4, illustrated how Vida's presence affected fans around the country—*and* the pressure that was starting to feed back to him from the very fact of his popularity.

When Blue was announced as the starting pitcher the day before a game with the California Angels in Anaheim, 44,000 avid spectators filled the baseball park to witness the new phenomenon. As is customary, fifteen minutes before the actual start of the game Blue stepped out of the Oakland dugout to start his warm-up with coach Vern Hoscheit, Oakland outfielder Curt Blefary, and pitching coach Bill Posedel.

Suddenly fans—thousands of them—began pouring out of the stands, waving their scorecards and autograph books in the air, all heading straight for Vida Blue at the first-base warm-up mound.

Manager Dick Williams spotted the danger first. "Take him to the bullpen and no visitors," he shouted from the dugout.

Posedel, Blefary, and Hoscheidt quickly formed a protective phalanx around Vida and escorted him out to the bullpen, where he could warm up in safety.

Vida won the game, 2–1.

So by the time the All-Star Game arrived Blue was being touted not only as the best rookie of the 1972 season, but perhaps the top rookie ever. For pitching comparisons, most critics measured him against Sandy Koufax, but even here the great Dodger southpaw was the one who suffered by comparisons. Koufax had struggled through three obscure major-league years before attaining his status as perhaps the best pitcher baseball had ever known. Control problems had kept him from realizing his full potential until he was a veteran of twenty-five years of age.

Blue, on the other hand, had seemingly reached a plateau of greatness in his first full year of major-league ball, at the age of twenty-two. Almost single-handed, he was helping Oakland hold onto a considerable lead in the American League West.

When he was named the American League's starting pitcher in the All-Star Game in Detroit, fans and journalists alike rubbed their hands in anticipation of seeing the six-foot 190-pounder with the sharply rising fast ball, the snapping curve, and the marvelous facility for keeping the ball hidden from view until the three-quarter-arm delivery was in its final moment of release.

By early July, All-Star time, Vida Blue was the most exciting baseball player to come along in years. The only question that remained was how far would he go. How would he match up against Baltimore this fall in the play-offs? How would he do in the World Series? What kind of dent would he make in the record books?

On the night of July 13 he faced the first of his tests in Detroit's Kezar Stadium, at the forty-second annual All-Star Game. He had been chosen to start for the American League, while the Pirates' Dock Ellis pitched for the National League—a precedent-shattering decision, in view of the fact that never before had two black pitchers faced each other as starters in a major-league All-Star Game.

In Detroit that night, during batting practice and before the National League batters had taken their first look at Vida, Henry Aaron said:

"I haven't hit against him yet. But don't talk to me about fast balls. They're not the test. When you talk about great left-handed pitchers I'll tell you about the day Sandy Koufax came into Atlanta to pitch against us and he had nothing . . . I mean he just had no fast ball that afternoon. So he went out, and he pitched with his head, and he pitched the curve and he gave us just two or three hits and shut us out.

"I'm not saying Vida Blue can't do that because I still haven't hit against him, and even after tonight I won't have seen him enough. I'm just saying that 'fast' is important, but by itself it isn't greatness."

But those who had seen Blue work were deeply impressed. "His fast ball jumps, bores in on the batter," said Yankee manager Ralph Houk. "Our guys tell me he's faster than anybody in our league but Sam McDowell, and he's as fast as Sam when he has to be."

"He rarely hurts himself," said Ted Williams, whose three-run homer in the ninth inning had won the All-Star Game here thirty years before. "If he walks somebody, he'll throw strikes after that. He throws hard consistently and has great control. The combination gives him command of the game."

Just two weeks shy of his twenty-second birthday, Vida was turning out to be just as fast with a quote as with a fast ball, as he relaxed at his hotel on the eve of the All-Star Game and fielded reporters' questions.

"My *repertoire*," he said, laughing at his own fancy vocabulary, "consists of three basic pitches—fast ball, curve ball, and let-up. I throw them all the same: left-handed."

Joe Cronin, president of the American League, asked him if he'd ever pitched against National League superstars like Hank Aaron, Roberto Clemente, and Willie Mays.

"No," Vida replied with a broad smile. "But if they hit the ball, I hope the guys hit the cutoff man."

Someone asked him if he'd ever seen Sandy Koufax, to whom people were constantly comparing Blue.

"No, I never saw Koufax pitch," he replied, "not in person or on TV. The only guy I used to try to imitate was Willie Mays—hitting."

Did he know that the American League had lost eight All-Star games in a row and hadn't won since 1962?

"Is that so?" asked Vida, sounding impressed. "Thanks for telling me. We'll try to do something about that tomorrow."

Besides testing his arm against the biggest bats in the National League, there were other reasons the game was important to Vida. For one, despite the fact that his name was on every tongue, the All-Star Game marked the first time that Blue would pitch a game on national television—in this case, before 58,000,000 viewers.

And then, of course, there was a chance for him to help break the American League's long-standing losing streak. The last time the American Leaguers had won had been two days after Vida's thirteenth birthday!

And Vida started out the game like a man with something to prove. In his first inning he threw only strikes and retired the side on seven pitches. The great Willie Mays, leading off for the Nationals, took one fast ball, then swung at the second, and grounded out to shortstop Luis Aparicio of the Red Sox. Slugger Hank Aaron of the Atlanta Braves batted next. He also watched one fast ball, then lunged for a curve and grounded out to third baseman Brooks Robinson. Then Joe Torre, the future major-league batting champ, came up to hit. The Cardinals' third baseman took one fast ball for a strike, fouled off another one, before popping up to second baseman Rod Carew of the Twins.

It was a fitting start for a pitcher whose 17 wins ranked as the most ever carried into an All-Star Game. (The previous high was Bob Feller's 16 wins in 1941.)

But in the end, the National League's power-packed lineup—combined with the short fences in that infamous Tiger Stadium—conspired to do Vida in—and almost everyone else who pitched that day.

Willie Stargell batted first for the NL in the second inning. Attempting to crowd the future National League home run champ, Vida's curve broke in too close, hitting Willie and giving him a free base. Next up, Johnny Bench pounded a Blue fast ball into the upper right-center-field seats to give the National League a 2–0 lead.

Vida got out of the inning without further damage, but he found trouble again in the third. With two out, Hank Aaron hit his first All-Star homer, rifling a drive into the upper deck in right field. Tiger Stadium, famed as a hitter's paradise, was living up to its reputation.

Home runs by Frank Robinson and Reggie Jackson eventually won the game for the American Leaguers. And Vida Blue became the youngest pitcher ever to win an All-Star Game.

After the game, National League manager Sparky Anderson said he thought that Vida "did an excellent job" and that the left-hander had showed "terrific poise" for a youngster playing in his first All-Star Game. However, he added: "I don't think I was seeing Vida Blue at his best. Or Dock Ellis either, for that matter. Both of them are so young and must have been under considerable pressure."

Said American League catcher Bill Freehan: "Blue only popped the ball two or three times. It seemed like he was trying to turn it over most of the time. But when he reached back, it was really there," Freehan added.

Before the start of the game, Vida had been asked to describe how he felt. "I'm scared stiff," he had replied with characteristic frankness. "I'm shaking." After the game, newsmen badgered him, trying to get him to comment on his performance.

Vida was slightly irritated, a state the newsmen

would get to know better as the second half of the season wore on. Sipping his habitual postgame Coke, Vida
finally said: "Look, these are the best guys in the
majors. This was the All-Star Game. What am I, a
super All-Star?"

And the answer, as far as the general baseball-loving
public was concerned, had to be "Yes!"

But ex-Yankee great Whitey Ford probed deeper into
Blue's performance after the All-Star Game: "You
could see he was nervous. You know he is much better
than he showed that night, and the way the wind was
blowing, you could hardly say he got bombed. But the
way he looks to me, I'd have to say that his up-and-
down performance was the best thing for him. If he
gets into a World Series now, he'll have left all that
nervousness behind him."

But for most fans and observers, the crucial question
was not whether Oakland would get to the World Series
and, if so, whether the A's would win. The tantalizing
question was not even if Vida Blue would win 20 games.
Instead, most people were asking how many over 20
he'd win. The strain of being twenty-one years old, with
a superstar aura forming around his head and the fate
of his entire ball club riding on his shoulders—Vida
had been able to hide it up to now. But with his bad
day against the National League superstars—despite
the excuses, none of which Vida himself ever accepted
—the tensions and strains soon became obvious in his
performance and later even in his personality.

7

Mounting Pressure

A few years previously Denny McLain had won 34 games—and Vida, 17-3 at the All-Star break, was far ahead of McLain's record-setting pace.

"He must get out there every fourth day," said McLain, explaining the tough-mindedness required to win 30. "Rain or shine, I was out there every fourth day. If there were two rainouts in a row, I'd get out there before someone else. You can't worry about offending anyone. In '68 I pitched the Sunday before the All-Star break and the first day after it. Every time you pitch a fifth day," McLain continued, "sooner or later that takes a start away from you. You've got to be out there forty times."

Naturally, the A's management, with the biggest drawing card ever in their fold, was thinking along the same lines. Shortly after the All-Star Game in Detroit the A's were faced with a situation in which Blue would work only once during an eight-game home stand and pitch only twice in twelve days, owing to days off in the schedule. So manager Dick Williams ordered Vida and Jim "Catfish" Hunter to switch turns in the rotation.

It was pointed out to Williams that by switching Blue and Hunter, the team was forcing Blue to miss his starting assignment scheduled for a Bat Day at home. Wouldn't that hurt the promotion?

Said Williams: "He's enough of a promotion by himself."

So far employer-employee relations between Finley and Blue had been amicable. But Vida had no illusions.

"Right now he treats me like I was a gift from God," Blue said. "But I'm not going to win every game I pitch. And things could change."

Early one morning Blue was awakened by a telephone call. The caller was Charlie O., and he had a peculiar request, an idea he believed was pure public relations genius. Finley wanted his bleary-eyed pitcher to change his legal name to "True Blue."

Vida refused. "He actually wanted me to change my name," he said, shaking his head in disbelief. Finley, according to Vida, had tried to "Bogart" him.

"Bogartin," Blue says, "is when a guy walks around like he owns the world or acts superior or pushes other people around. I've seen guys go and get cocky like that. I don't think it's the way to be.

"I can't read the newspaper without seeing my

name," he added, listing the temptations to "Bogartin" sudden success had afforded *him*. "But I've got to be modest about the whole thing. I'll tell you a guy who's great and modest at the same time—Brooks Robinson. That's my man."

One particularly irritating manifestation of his success was the harassment and invasion of his privacy by the groupies that afflict every performer in the limelight. But Vida was managing to keep his private life under control.

"I guess you could call me a square," Blue said. "I don't usually go out more than three or four times during a two-week road trip. I do okay with women. But most of the time I'd just rather get me a bottle of soda and a paper, watch some TV, and go to bed."

Making his adjustment to big-league and big-city life easier, there had been very few racial incidents to scar his life, either before coming to the big leagues or after. But he recalled one incident at the beginning of the season, in Anaheim, when a waitress tactlessly addressed him as "boy."

"I got mad as hell," he recalls. "But then she started to cry like crazy, and I saw how stupid the whole thing was."

After the All-Star break, with the pressure steadily mounting as fans came to expect a perfect effort from Vida each and every time out, Blue slumped dramatically to a 7-5 record, winning only one game in September.

"For a while," said teammate Sal Bando, "I think he lost some of his confidence. He lost a couple of games back to back, and he started doubting himself. He wasn't throwing the ball as hard.

"Guys got hits who didn't come close to getting hits earlier. Guys got hits with two strikes, and that hadn't happened much earlier. I think that he was just tired mentally and physically.

"He changed, too," Bando added. "The fame changed him some. He became more of a loner. He didn't talk to so many people. He had his own thoughts, his own problems. He wasn't so carefree as when he first started."

After taking his eighteenth win from the Angels, Vida beat the Detroit Tigers for his nineteenth. As his victories piled up, so did demands for interviews, requests for special appearances, and pleas for special favors. The impact of becoming a national hero proved unbalancing for a twenty-one-year-old. Just the phone ringing a hundred times a day was unnerving enough. Vida began to dread talking to reporters, especially before each of the three games in which he tried unsuccessfully to win No. 20. He even compiled a list of the ten questions he hated the most.

Vida went out for his first shot at win No. 20 against the Cleveland Indians on July 28, two days after his twenty-second birthday. He lost, 4–1.

His second try for victory No. 20 was against Kansas City on August 3. After five innings, and five runs, he was lifted for a reliever. He was saved from defeat by a late-inning A's rally, but that twentieth win remained as elusive as ever.

And the pressure was still building.

"I'm almost crazy from the pressure," Vida complained in the clubhouse after the game against the Royals. "Mercy, mercy, mercy me," he wailed, "this was the toughest of them all. Everybody wants to know if I'm going to win twenty. That's where all the pressure is coming from," he added. "I felt good when I went out there, I thought I had my usual stuff."

The night before he went out for No. 20 for the fourth time he talked to reporters about what that magic number meant for him. "Even if I don't pitch any better, it will be better for me mentally to get over this," Vida said. "Over the years when you've rated pitchers, there's been a lot of attention paid to the first pitcher who's going to win twenty, a lot of pressure."

Before the effects of the pressure really surfaced, however, Vida stole his critics' thunder. On August 7, pitching against Joel Horlen, he shut out the Chicago White Sox, 1–0, on five hits, becoming the first pitcher in either league to win 20 games. He struck out six, including two in the ninth, while walking only two batters.

Vida was ecstatic. Finley was overjoyed. Fans all over the country felt vindicated, seeing their carefully invested tickets to see Vida pitch return a 20-game dividend.

"I started shaking in the ninth inning," he said after the game, "because I wanted to win so much."

"He throws a heavy fast ball," said the White Sox's eventual American League home run champ Bill Melton. "It either swoops away from you or sinks like a rock. Sam McDowell," he added, "has a light fast ball that kind of floats past you. That's why I think Vida's is better."

"Anytime a new phenom comes along," said White Sox pitching coach Johnny Sain, in his prime one of the National League's all-time greats, "the hitters don't take him too seriously. It seems as if he has more stuff than he really does. But after a while, the hitters zero in on him and the pitcher has to prove himself all over again. It's obvious," he added, "that Blue is proving himself."

Thus he became the A's first pitcher to win 20 games in one season since Bobby Shantz did it for the Philadelphia Athletics back in 1952. It was Vida's eighteenth complete game and eighth shutout.

After he won that twentieth game, newsmen gathered around Vida for an interview that the reporters would subsequently classify as "hostile." Someone asked Vida if winning his twentieth would remove "the monkey from your back."

"There was no monkey on my back," Vida answered. "There just was the pressure, that pressure."

Vida was poker-faced, holding his head between his hands.

Another reporter asked Blue if he'd add another dime to the two he habitually carried in his back pocket (one for every 10 games won), implying that his goal should now be 30 victories.

"There you go again," Vida replied angrily, banging the table with his hand. "There's that damn pressure."

Manager Dick Williams said Blue had had an upset stomach before the game. It was a combination of nerves and something Vida had eaten. It had bothered him throughout.

"I started shaking in the ninth inning because I wanted to win so bad," Vida added. "I took three Alka-Seltzers during the game. That's how shaky I was."

Normally this twentieth game would have been the high point of any pitcher's season. But the demands of fans, management, and the press were insatiable. Throughout the season, up to the All-Star break, Vida had made winning look so easy that fans had begun to take his victories for granted. Twenty wins was a milestone, they agreed, but certainly not the goal. How many games would he win? Would he surpass Mc-Lain's record high of 34?

It looked easy, but of course it wasn't with pressure on the field and harassment off it. Still, he performed amazingly well. In his next two starts he pitched four-hitters, but came up with two 1–0 losses, to the Red Sox's Gary Peters and to the Yankees' Mel Stottlemyre.

Then came a week to remember for Vida and the other Athletics. It started with a four-game sweep over the Red Sox at Fenway Park; it ended with a fifteen-minute meeting with President Nixon at the White House.

As the week opened, Vida found himself facing Red Sox pitcher Sonny Siebert. Siebert himself was en route to a 20-game season, and one of his conquests had been Vida Blue, beating him in a tight duel back on May 28. The Red Sox, in fact, were the only team Vida hadn't defeated.

Pitching the second game of a doubleheader, Vida

needed ten innings and great relief help from Darold
Knowles to earn a 5–3 triumph, but he hung in long
enough to both avenge his defeat by Siebert—and
notch his twenty-first victory of the season.

Four days later, in Yankee Stadium, before 50,507
spectators, Blue pitched and batted his way to victory
No. 22 on "Blue Sunday." He drove in the game's first
run with a bunt single, fell behind, 4–2, when the
Yankees scored all their runs in the bottom of the
seventh, and bunt-singled with the bases loaded in the
top of the eighth as the A's scored four runs to win,
6–4.

And the pressure was still building.

"Physically I feel okay," he told reporters after the
game, "but mentally I'm about to crack up. I'm feeling the effects of the pressure from the press, radio,
and TV. I've been feeling it for months. Everything
about today's game was pressure for me.

"I'm hoping," he added, "that as time goes on, the
pressure will wear off. I want to go to the movies and
not be seen. Most of the time I lock myself in my room
so I won't feel any pressure."

The next day Vida got up early to appear on NBC's
Today show. By midmorning *Time* magazine was on
the stands featuring Blue on the cover. That evening it
was ABC's turn at Vida, who appeared on the *Dick
Cavett Show* with Cleveland Hall-of-Famer Bob Feller.
When Vida returned to the backstage room where other
guests and staff members were watching a TV monitor,
even the stagehands applauded his performance. Next
he was off to Washington and the White House, for

what turned out to be an enjoyable interview with the President.

The day started out ominously. The bus scheduled to take the team to the White House never appeared, so the A's who had received Presidential invitations left the hotel five to a cab. Then the President arrived an hour and forty-five minutes late—owing, he explained, to an extended Cabinet meeting.

The encounter took place in the President's Oval Office. For openers, Dick Nixon and Dick Williams had a short conversation. Then Williams introduced his ballplayers to the President.

In response to Nixon's conventional grip, Vida gave the President a "soul handshake." "That's the way *we* do it," Blue said.

"I'll give you a challenge," Nixon countered. "Every year until you reach thirty, you've got to win as many ball games as your age that season."

Later the President posed in the middle of a group photograph. Holding an Oakland Athletics' green-and-gold cap presented to him by Vida Blue, he was caught for posterity shaking Vida's hand.

"They're not going to like this in Baltimore," Nixon quipped.

Team captain Sal Bando asked the President whether the wage freeze meant that owner Finley wouldn't be able to give his players raises.

"Well," said Nixon, turning to Blue and pointing over toward Finley, "it means that he can't give you more gas for your car.

"I've read you're the most underpaid player in baseball," added Nixon. "I wouldn't like to be the Oakland lawyer negotiating your next contract."

Later on Vida was to use those words for ammunition in his salary fight with Finley.

On August 29 Blue was breezing along into the ninth inning with a five-hitter and a 4–1 lead over Washington when Tim Cullen cracked a two-run homer to cut the margin to 4–3. But Blue hung on to get pinch-hitter Don Mincher to fly out to Rick Monday for the final out and raise his record to 23-7. Blue had given up 6 hits but had struck out 10, defeating the Senators in the first game of a double header.

It had been a fairy tale week, in which the youth from a Louisiana mill town had chatted face to face with the man who holds the most powerful political office in the entire world. The memory of the meeting shimmered, then dissolved like a mirage, as Vida managed only one victory in his next six starts.

Blue was beaten 2–1 by Minnesota, despite the fact that he'd struck out 12 Twins. Next he fell to the Angels, 6–1. Against the power-hitting Twins again, Vida gave up 7 hits and 5 runs (three of them unearned) to lose, 7–5. The 6 bases on balls he gave up were his per-game high for the season. And in two other games he wasn't the pitcher of record.

Meanwhile, the rest of the Athletics were jubilant. On September 15 they had defeated the Chicago White Sox to clinch the American League West title— and a share of the play-off money.

8

No Peace Anywhere

Vida Blue tucked his shirt into orange-colored trousers. "I'm sorry," he said. "I'm not supposed to talk baseball. I won't even be out there for a night or two."

His face was solemn, tense. His mouth was grim, his lips compressed with no room for a smile.

"Vida," someone said, "you've been losing. What's—"

"It's not my arm," Blue cut in. "It's my body . . . the pressure. Everybody thinks I should win every time I go out there. I'm tired. I. . . ." He paused—a long provocative silence, then: "I'm not supposed to talk baseball." His eyes were fixed blankly on the dressing-room exit.

"The pressure," Blue mumbled again.

"Catfish Hunter loses games," someone volunteered,

trying to lighten the tension caused by Vida's six straight starts without a victory.

Blue stared at the reporter hard. "Yeah," he said finally. "Catfish loses sometimes, but people don't notice. They only notice when Vida Blue loses."

His Oakland teammates naturally sympathized with Vida when the pressure of publicity began to pile up on his sagging shoulders. On at least one occasion Reggie Jackson (who had endured the same syndrome, although to a lesser degree, a few years before when he went on a home run binge) pleaded with reporters to leave Blue alone.

Baltimore pitcher Dave McNally, also a 20-game winner, commented: "Can you imagine having all that publicity in what amounts to your first year? Even worse, can you imagine having it at the age of twenty-two?"

In any case, the personality metamorphosis was complete. The smiling, witty Blue who had playfully fielded reporters' questions with a put-on innocence before the All-Star Game had turned into a sullen, difficult man. Whereas his original attitude and humor had led to comparisons with comedian Flip Wilson, Blue seemed more and more to resemble Greta Garbo as the play-offs for the American League title (and the chance to go to the World Series) opened against Baltimore.

Of course, the pressure had been building long before the All-Star Game. Each victory had meant additional pressure—each interview, each request for an interview. Wherever he went fans flocked to see him pitch. A total of 2,140,000 fans saw the A's play at home and on the road, with nearly half—910,000—showing up for games Blue pitched. And wherever he went, people made demands on his time and his attention.

"Friends I didn't know I had kept popping up," he said. "There were too many of them—from my hometown, my home state, my high school, people I met in the meat market. People were always saying, 'If you need anything, call me,' but I'm not impressed with them."

Then there were the incessant interviews from the news and communications media, large and small, from near and far, calling him day and night. Meanwhile, Vida was trying to win ball games, to enhance his own stature and bring Charlie Finley a pennant. Few athletes have ever experienced such intensity of pressure—the kind that Roger Maris felt in 1961, when he was hitting 61 home runs, the pressure Denny McLain knew in 1968, when he was winning 34 games.

"It's tough," said Sandy Koufax, a man who knows and understands the meaning of pressure and its effects on the mental state of a pitcher. "It seems like you have no peace. There's an incredible amount of pressure put on these days with television and the fact that there's so much coverage. And there's even more pressure on the field for a pitcher because you have a special feeling of responsibility. You don't go out there every day, but when you do, you're charged with winning or losing, and when you lose, you've got to wait four days to get another chance at it."

Of course, Koufax had been the last left-hander before Blue to dominate the hitters completely, so comparisons between the two were inevitable. In his funnier moments, Blue used to respond to the mention of Koufax's name by saying, "Funny, I don't look Jewish." Nevertheless, he was flattered by the comparisons between himself and the former Dodger ace who was forced out of baseball at the peak of his career by an arthritic elbow.

In comparing the two left-handers, only the second half of Koufax's career is relevant. During the first half Sandy was a fast ball pitcher with an inbuilt and stubborn wild streak, who was too unpredictable to win consistently. It took him seven years to gain the control that Blue got in three minor-league seasons.

"There's a big difference in our two cases," said Koufax, who began pitching in the majors at nineteen. "He probably was much more advanced when he started than I was. I really didn't play that much baseball as a kid, and I did very little pitching. I didn't pitch in high school, and I pitched seven or eight games in college and four or five in sandlot ball. That was it. The next year I was in the majors, but even then I didn't pitch. I spent the first two years sitting on the bench as a bonus player. I don't think there's anything that can retard you more than sitting there and not getting a chance to pitch.

"In addition to his good fast ball," Koufax added, "his control is the biggest thing he has going for him. He doesn't walk too many batters, but that's not the only thing. He hits the inside corner, and he hits the outside corner with regularity. That can't be happening by accident.

"He doesn't have as good control of his curve, but on days when he gets it over, he's going to have an outstanding day, and when he doesn't get it over, he'll still have a good chance because of his fast ball and control. He's also strong, and he holds his stuff well. He doesn't lose it as the game goes on."

Bill Posedel, Oakland's pitching coach, explained another aspect of Blue's talent for throwing the ball by batters. "He has this extra flick of the wrist," said Posedel. "You get the idea that his motion is all through; then he gets this extra snap on the pitch. He isn't just a strong arm. He's more than that. That's what makes him special. Lots of guys throw hard. Vida has that something else. It's the difference."

Batters around the league, meanwhile, claimed that the difference was the way Blue's fast ball approached the plate. According to baseball's all-time authority on the art of hitting, Ted Williams—who had confronted and blasted out of the park some of the finest fast balls ever thrown—Blue's fast ball "either swoops away or sinks in rapidly on you. When a batter makes contact, he's hitting something dead."

"I just can't get excited about all the statistics, attention, and publicity," Blue himself said. "It's a weird scene. You win a few baseball games, and all of a sudden you're surrounded by reporters and TV men with cameras, asking you about Vietnam and race relations and stuff about yourself. Man, I'm only a kid. I don't know exactly who I am. I don't have a whole philosophy of life set down."

"I know what it's like," said teammate Reggie Jackson. "I've been there . . . I tried to be real nice to everybody, but everybody's looking to jump you. But Vida'll be able to handle it better than I did," he added. "I'm much more tense, high-strung. He's calmer, a cool cookie. Vida acts like he's been around a lot longer than he has."

In any case, in his final start of the regular season, Vida shut out the Milwaukee Brewers, 7–0, for his twenty-fourth victory against eight losses.

9

Losing the Play-off

The play-off between Oakland and the Baltimore Orioles for the American League title excited the interest of fans and press throughout the country. The Orioles, with a pitching staff of four 20-game winners and an All-Star lineup including all-time greats, were favorites to win not only their league's pennant, but the World Series, no matter what opposition the National League provided them. The only conceivable stumbling block was Vida Blue. And he was scheduled to pitch the opening game in Baltimore.

The city had a carnival air that week, with fans making the pilgrimage from the farthest reaches of the nation. Hotel clerks wore straw hats, with yellow buttons pinned to their lapels that shrieked: "Smile, you're in Baltimore." Charlie Finley arrived in town at the head of his Oakland entourage, his stocky torso wrapped in a double-knit Pucci sport coat. When asked to pinpoint its color, he replied, "Why, it's Vida Blue, naturally."

Even the rain that forced a one-day postponement of the opener couldn't dampen the rampant enthusiasm. It was Mardi Gras in New Orleans, Carnival in Rio, and the Fourth of July rolled into one—for everyone except Vida Blue.

Leaving a meeting of Williams and the A's held behind closed doors at a hotel in downtown Baltimore, the twenty-two-year-old 24-game winner knew better than fans and press that he had to defeat Baltimore in that opening game if underdog Oakland were to stand a chance in the play-off series. The pressure, as Black Hawk goalie Tony Esposito was later to say in another play-off context, was unreal.

"How do you feel about starting against the Orioles?" a reporter asked Vida in the lobby outside the meeting room.

Blue kept on walking, his eyes focused in front of him. "I'll just go out there and pitch," he replied, his mouth set in a grim line. "If they hit the ball, they hit it. If they don't, they don't. Don't ask me any more questions because I want to go back to my hotel and get some sleep."

"Why won't you answer any more questions?" asked another newsman.

"I have my reasons," Vida replied with a barely repressed anger. "Vida Blue reasons."

After Vida left, manager Dick Williams defended Vida against the reporters' accusation that Blue was uncooperative with the press. Williams said that Vida had held up well throughout the season while bearing an enormous burden of responsibility. Win or lose, Williams added, Vida would be available to writers immediately after every play-off appearance. However, on the days his pitchers were scheduled to start, Williams insisted, the writers were to stay away from them.

"That Oriole lineup is pressure enough," Williams said, "without having to pitch to you guys, too."

According to other sources, though, the real reason for Vida's anger had to do with a gossip item which had appeared in a national Sunday supplement. During an interview set up in question-and-answer form, Vida had been asked whether he was currently dating a white or black girlfriend. The writer, who was not a sportswriter, stated parenthetically that Vida's girlfriend was white.

"I don't know whether that's what's put him out," said roommate Tommy Davis. "But if that's what it is, I don't blame him one bit. What business is it of anyone? He goes out with a number of girls. Maybe his girlfriend is chartreuse, who knows? Who keeps track? He gets an awful lot of calls."

Twenty-four hours later, under clear skies and on a field at Baltimore Memorial Stadium transformed by rain and the Baltimore Colts into a fenced-in marshland, Vida Blue prepared to take on the Oriole machine in the year's most dramatic encounter.

Starting against Baltimore 20-game winner Dave McNally, Blue was invincible for the first three innings. "He was throwing so hard those first few innings," said Oriole center fielder Paul Blair, "that it seemed his fast ball was moving a foot and a half just as we started to swing. It was entirely too tough to hit.

"But," Blair added, "we started talking on the bench and everybody was advising everyone else to lay off that rising fast ball. The idea was to give it a chance to rise right out of the strike zone. Manager Earl Weaver had been saying it all the time, but we had to see it for ourselves."

And suddenly Vida began to find himself pitching into an endless succession of 3-and-2 counts.

Blair went up to the plate again—his lifetime record against Vida Blue now 0 for 11. "I decided to try something different to get around his speed," Blair recalled later. For the first time against Blue, Blair inched his hands up the bat, choking it. "I never remember choking up on the wood before," he said, "but I realized it was the only way I could hit him. I choked up about two inches."

His new tactic paid a swift dividend. On Vida's second pitch, Blair stroked the ball into the left-field corner for a two-run double that gave the Orioles a 5–3 victory.

Blue (and McNally in the Oakland half) was lifted in that disastrous four-run seventh inning, although after the game the Orioles were unanimous that he had never lost his top form at any time throughout the game. A couple of mistakes, plus smart Oriole tactics, they argued—not the pressure—had caused Vida's downfall.

Typically, after the game Vida received more attention from the press than any of the winning Orioles. And he placed the blame for his defeat squarely on his own shoulders—as he had admitted laying the tack trap years ago in his Mansfield grammar school.

Analyzing the seventh-inning Baltimore explosion, Vida offered no excuses. Although the Orioles had scored four times when there were already two outs, Vida said he felt he'd thrown just one bad pitch—a high and inside fast ball that pinch-hitter Curt Motton had slammed for a double.

Vida also admitted making a mistake in the fourth inning on a pitch that Baltimore slugger Boog Powell hit to left field for a run-scoring single.

Still, no Oriole had got more than one hit. And Vida had struck out Powell, Merv Rettenmund (the club's leading batter), and superstar Frank Robinson twice each.

In fact, in the Oriole clubhouse Frank Robinson was marveling at Blue's speed, even in defeat. "I whiffed twice and walked once in four tries," he exclaimed. "Nobody will ever make a living hitting off that guy." Then Frank turned exuberant. "We beat their big guy!" he announced. "They gotta feel down. We beat their main man."

He was right. The A's felt "down" and played the way they felt. Baltimore swept the next two games and the series.

10

Playing It Cool

After Oakland lost the play-off series to Baltimore, Vida closed up the apartment he shared with first baseman/outfielder Tommy Davis and returned to Mansfield. He was tired, physically and mentally. He needed the warmth of his family; he needed the uncritical acceptance only lifelong friends are prepared to offer. And most of all, he wanted to escape for a time relentless media eyes that had followed him incessantly throughout the season, interfering with his private life, his sleep—and even, perhaps, his pitching.

But for the man who had drawn 1,000,000 fans through the turnstiles on days he was scheduled to pitch there was to be no escape from publicity. Shortly after he returned home to Mansfield, the twenty-four-man committee of the Baseball Writers' Association sat down to choose the recipient of the Cy Young Award, traditionally presented to the best pitchers in the American and National Leagues. The Chicago Cubs' Ferguson Jenkins won over the Mets' Tom Seaver in the National League. And in the American League, the committee's overwhelming choice was Vida Blue. Vida received fourteen first-place votes to nine for Detroit Tiger 20-game winner Mickey Lolich. Vida was the only player named on all twenty-four ballots.

Thus, Vida—at twenty-two—became the youngest recipient of the award ever, displacing Dean Chance, who had won as a twenty-three-year-old with the California Angels in 1964.

And naturally, with the exciting Vida Blue involved, the award generated its share of controversy. Ironically enough, Vida started it.

"I really thought Mickey Lolich would win it," said Vida, with the candor that had become his personal hallmark. "If I participated in the voting," he added, "I'd have voted for Lolich.

"What am I going to do for an encore?" Vida asked himself even before the question was put to him. "Just keep trying to win. The most important thing in my life is to win."

Lolich fans were quick to back up Vida's vote of confidence in Mickey with their own statistics. Lolich, they pointed out, had won 25 games, one more than Vida.

And Lolich had *lost* 14 games, Blue backers countered, while Vida had lost only 8.

Lolich-ites argued that their man had pitched 376 innings (high for the major leagues) to Vida's 312.

Lolich was the strikeout king, with 308 to 301 for Blue. Lolich pitched 29 complete games, while Vida pitched 24.

But the logic of Blue's choice over Lolich rested finally on one overwhelming statistic. Mickey Lolich's earned run average was a reasonable 2.92. Vida's ERA was an astounding 1.82. And Vida had led the crowds through the turnstiles, and Vida had led his team to a pennant.

With these arguments in his favor—and the Cy Young trophy in his living room—Vida sat back and waited for the results of the Most Valuable Player voting. These two awards—if he could manage to collar the second—would increase his bargaining power when he sat down with Charlie O. to negotiate a new contract. Vida had already engaged a lawyer, Los Angeles attorney Robert Gerst. On Gerst's advice, Vida decided to wait for the MVP announcement before starting salary negotiations.

Vida's selection as the American League's MVP also stirred up discontent. In becoming only the second pitcher ever in the American League to win both awards, Vida outdistanced another Oakland teammate in the MVP balloting, the A's team captain and third baseman, Sal Bando. Vida's victory over Bando revived a longtime baseball dispute over whether pitchers should be eligible for *both* the Cy Young and MVP awards.

"After all," said Bando, "we're not eligible for the Cy Young Award, so why should a pitcher be able to take home the MVP? And let's face it," he added. "No matter how good the pitcher is, he's only going to be out there one-fourth of the time."

Vida's reply was swift and to the point. "Pitchers are in the league, right?" he said. "That makes us eligible." Diplomatically, he added: "Not only is this a personal thing, it's a team thing. Anyway, I thought either Reggie Jackson or Bando would get it from our team," he continued. "They really helped our team. It wasn't a superyear for either one of them compared to other years they've had in the majors," he added, "but they were really valuable to us."

Of course, the value of the award to Vida was as a wedge to pry open Charlie Finley's bank vault. Blue, under advice from his attorney, had already decided to ask for $100,000 in 1972. Right now, though, with a long winter ahead of him, he was playing it cool. And so was Charlie Finley.

"I can't tell you how much I'm going to pay Vida Blue next season because I don't know myself," Finley said shortly after Blue received the second of his two awards. "I don't even know how much the government, with the wage freeze and all, will allow me to pay him."

At the time, it seemed a straightforward, innocent statement. In retrospect, though, it's obvious that Finley, a skilled, if controversial, corporate negotiator in his own right, was beginning to tighten his purse strings.

"Some people," he added, "think that because Vida had a 17-2 record by the All-Star break and a 7-6 record after it [in fact, Vida's totals were actually 17-3 and 7-5] that perhaps he lost some of his box-office magic."

Finley paused, letting the notion of Blue's late-season fade in popularity sink into his listeners' heads. Then he continued with a mild disclaimer, "I would like to think that such was not the case. Vida's overall record for 1971 was outstanding. It was verified by the fact that he won these two awards."

Finley paused again. "I have to admit that his drawing power in Oakland subsided as the season drew to a close," he reiterated purposefully. "And that's hard to understand."

It was a clever speech. While ostensibly praising Vida, Finley had managed at the same time to damn him, insinuating that halfway through the season Vida's magic at the turnstiles had worn off. In praising him, of course, he had failed to mention that Vida had brought the A's their first pennant in forty years, that Vida had attracted an average of 10,000 extra fans to the ball park every time he pitched—that Vida had been paid for all this a paltry $16,000, a Cadillac, and some gas company credit cards.

But the weakest link in Finley's chain of subtle accusation was the very one he himself had—with a shrewd debater's technique—mildly rejected. In 1971, the A's had drawn 914,993 to their games. This represented an increase of 136,638 over 1970, when Blue was in Des Moines for all but the month of September. Furthermore, the distribution of Oakland's attendance peaks proved conclusively that Blue was the reason the Oakland turnstiles had started to creak with increased regularity. The A's exceeded the 20,000 mark sixteen times in Oakland, with Blue the starting pitcher in ten of those sixteen games. And in the eighteen games in which the Athletics drew 5,000 or less, Vida had pitched only twice.

Vida's contribution on the road was even more convincing. Six times away from home the Oakland A's played before crowds larger than 40,000. Vida Blue started every one of those games. Thirteen times the A's played in front of crowds larger than 30,000; Vida Blue started ten of those games.

The contract dispute between Charles O. Finley and Vida Blue that began soon after Vida won the Most Valuable Player award was to keep Vida's name in headlines through the winter, spring training, and right into the 1972 baseball season (temporarily preempted, of course, by the major-league players' pension strike). The argument was ostensibly over dollars and cents; Blue was asking, through attorney Robert Gerst, for $92,500. Charlie Finley was willing to pay not a cent more than $50,000.

To most observers, the implications of the dispute between this ballplayer and owner were far-reaching. At its farthest extension, the argument touched upon the fundamental structure of baseball itself—a game in which (by Congressional exemption from antitrust laws) an organization owns the rights to a man's labor for as long as he practices his profession. In fact, the argument was over baseball's controversial reserve clause; it was about professional negotiators hired by athletes; it was about the very nature of the game— whether baseball was a "national pastime" or a highly lucrative commercial enterprise.

All the elements of Finley's future bargaining position surfaced in an interview he gave to the Associated Press on February 26, 1972. By that time Blue remained the only Oakland ballplayer unsigned for the upcoming season. Reviewing the state of negotiations up to then, Finley said:

"Blue and Gerst came to Chicago January 8 to attend the Diamond Dinner. We met, and Gerst said Blue's asking price was $92,000. The original was $115,000. I said I would stand for $45,000. An hour later I raised it to $50,000.

"I want to explain the finance structure as I see it," Finley added. "Baseball has a rule that a salary can be cut a maximum of 20 percent the year or a total of 30 percent over two years. Say that Vida got $92,000 in 1972. Say he had a bad year and I cut him 20 percent. That would guarantee him no less than $73,600 in 1973. In 1973 he also was not too good. So in 1974 I cut him 10 percent. That makes it $66,240," Finley said. "Now, you add all those three years up and you come out with $231,840. You must stick with him during those three years hoping he will be all right. And all this doesn't take into account that he might develop a sore arm, break a leg or something, and would be lost.

"No," Finley said. "Based on the fact that Vida has had only one full year in the majors—and in my opinion it takes more than one year for a ballplayer to prove himself—I think $50,000 is a very, very fair offer."

He also said: "And I don't like the threats I've been

reading that Vida is going to play baseball in Japan. This is Gerst talking, not Vida Blue."

If at this late date, with the season opener less than a month and a half away, Finley thought he could afford to take a hard negotiating line, it was with good reason. He was already holding a trump card, and nine days later he laid it on the bargaining table. He invoked baseball's reserve clause.

In pro football, if there's a dispute between a player and management, the rules allow the player to play out his option—that is, to play without a contract for one season, after which (at least in theory) he becomes a free agent, able to sign with the club that bids most for his services. Not so in baseball, where a player is tied to a specific club—the one he originally signed with—for the duration of his playing career. Curt Flood, the ex-Cardinal and Senator superstar, was at this very time challenging the legality of the reserve clause before the U.S. Supreme Court, suing baseball for $4,100,000 damages as a result of being kept in professional bondage.

Still, at a time when many owners were badgering Finley to avoid further controversy by meeting Blue's demands, on March 8 Charlie O. sent Vida a formal letter of renewal, setting unilaterally the pitcher's '72 salary at $50,000.

Now Vida only had one option. With his contract already renewed by law and at the salary Finley had decreed, Vida's alternative to playing was to quit baseball.

11

Oh, Charlie O.!

"I won't trade or sell him," said Finley adamantly. "I stand by what I said. He plays for Oakland or he plays for nobody!"

Said lawyer Gerst in reply: "Past history indicates that Charlie needs to control and dictate everything and everyone connected with his organization. The irony of it all is Finley has said that if a man can't perform, he'll get rid of him. That's why he's had ten managers in the last ten years. But when he really gets someone who performs, he's unwilling to pay the top price. I think that's unfair, because a man who demands perfection from everyone else he hires should be willing to pay for it."

Gerst, of course, had already "accepted" Finley's $50,000, but with one counterprovision: that Vida automatically become a free agent at the end of the 1972 season. This would have meant the end of the

114

reserve clause, and Finley rejected the proposal as "absurd."

According to Gerst, Finley's final offer was made with one assumption in mind. "The insurance man," Gerst said, referring to the business in which Finley had made his millions, "told me he doesn't believe Vida has the guts to sit it out. 'Vida will cave in after a few days of spring training,' " Gerst claims Finley told him.

Gerst went on to say that he and Vida had decided on $92,000 as a fair salary after averaging out the salaries of eight of the best pitchers in baseball: Bob Gibson, Ferguson Jenkins, Juan Marichal, Tom Seaver, Dave McNally, Jim Palmer, and the Perry brothers, Gaylord and Jim. "Don't tell me that Vida isn't in that class," Gerst added. "I told Finley he'd get back the difference the first few times Vida pitched, and he'd have a happy and satisfied pitcher. Finley admitted Vida deserves it, but he said he wouldn't pay it, and that's the thing Vida keeps repeating, and it's driven him up the wall."

If Blue was hurting, he certainly managed to disguise it. With the press, he was his old self—constantly joking, poking fun not only at Finley, but at himself. During the winter he took time off to tour American bases in Vietnam with entertainer Bob Hope.

"If Finley insists that you play, what can you do about it?" Hope would ask him.

"If I have to play, I'll play," replied Vida. "But there's nothing in the reserve clause that says I can't pitch right-handed."

If Finley expected—as Gerst charged—that Vida would crack when spring training camps opened, he was wrong. Vida stayed home in Mansfield. And the sympathy—at this point—at the A's Mesa, Arizona, training site wasn't all for Finley.

"Let's face it," said slugger Reggie Jackson, who himself had held out after his 47-home run season in 1970, "there are name holdouts every year. But Vida is a horse of a different color. He's in a class by himself. He's the hottest thing to hit the game since Sandy Koufax.

"Vida puts people in the park," Jackson added, "and since he's a pitcher, you can measure it. People come out to see the long-ball hitters, too, but you never know how many. A fan might say, 'Well, I can't get out to see him on Friday, so I'll go on Sunday.' Vida's value in gate receipts is immense, and that gives him great bargaining power. There's no question he's worth ninety thousand dollars in terms of what he has done for the club."

There were some strange moments, too. According to Charlie Finley, on the afternoon of March 19, he just "happened" to be looking through binoculars from his twenty-fifth floor lakeside apartment in Oakland, when who should he see but Vida Blue, jogging around Lake Merritt. Finley shouted to Blue (with, we suppose, lung power that would have made Elvis Presley in his prime look like chronic laryngitis), and Blue (with eyesight as acute as Superman's) spotted Finley and waved back.

"After the fourth time around," said Finley, "Vida

came up and took a shower in my apartment. We sat around and watched a basketball game on TV."

They also ate some ice cream, which Finley said Blue had run down to purchase.

However this strange meeting came about, it ended in stalemate. Said Robert Gerst (who claimed that Finley had paid for the ice cream, not Blue): "It's the seduction of the young and innocent. Finley offered ice cream, and that's all. Vida took it and escaped with his virginity."

Meanwhile, odd events were taking place elsewhere. Militant blacks were beginning to grumble that there were racial overtones to Finley's reluctance to meet Vida's salary demands. The Oakland Black Caucus, a group claiming 500 members, declared it would urge black baseball fans to boycott Oakland games if Blue were "forced" to sit out the season. Elijah Turner, co-chairman of the organization, charged that Finley had displayed a "plantation mentality" in his negotiations with Blue.

Other fans, black and white, were equally concerned when the A's announced the release of Vida's room-mate, Tommy Davis. Two years the National League batting champ (with the Los Angeles Dodgers in 1962 and 1963), the thirty-three-year-old vet had performed dual roles for Vida throughout the '71 season. On the one hand, he was a private secretary, screening calls, protecting Vida's privacy. On the other, he was a den-mother-in-residence, constantly soothing Vida's frayed nerves.

Davis was closemouthed about his release from the

A's organization, perhaps fearful that a controversy would hurt his chances of latching on to another major-league club. Vida was equally noncommittal in his comments about his flute-playing ex-roomie. "I understand the club was dissatisfied with his performance at first base," was all he would say.

After the "Ice Cream Social" came "The Bathroom Farce." At a press conference held in Oakland, Vida Blue announced that he was quitting baseball to go to work for Dura Steel Company, whose top-selling product was a bathroom cabinet called Over-John which "holds 32 rolls of toilet paper. You need one, everyone needs one. . . ."

Wearing slacks, a striped shirt, and sneakers, Vida giggled when he made his formal retirement announcement. "Excuse me for smiling, but I am dead serious," said Vida. "This is a wonderful opportunity for me and one I feel I should take. It is with deep regret and sadness," he added, "that I announce my leaving baseball. I had hoped my career could have been longer. While it was short, it was packed with excitement."

Vida giggled again, whether from nervousness or from a fine sense of the absurd onlookers were unable to determine.

From Chicago, Charlie Finley also was playing it with a barely straight face. "I'm sorry to learn that Vida has decided to retire from baseball," Finley said. "He had a great year and had a great future ahead of him. As long as he is retiring," Finley added with thinly disguised sarcasm, "I'm happy that he has selected the steel industry and is starting out as vice-president. I personally spent five years with the U.S. Steel Corporation in Gary, Indiana," he continued, with the sarcasm now blatant, "the first four years serving my apprenticeship in a machine shop."

Vida's salary with Dura Steel was reported to be higher than the $50,000 Finley had offered him. And even if Vida and Charlie O. weren't taking the whole affair too seriously, Earl Epstein, president of Dura Steel, was dead sober when he said: "Vida will be calling on people without salesmen. . . . He'll be trouble-shooting, calling customers with problems: 'Hey, babe. You gotta problem? It's Vida.' Most people we deal with are sports nuts," Epstein added. "Middle Americans, very interested in sports."

Nevertheless, Epstein admitted, Vida had not signed a contract with his firm. Employment would be on a week-to-week basis. And, Robert Gerst pointed out, whatever advance on his services Vida had received, Epstein had already gained cash value in publicity by the mere fact of Blue's press conference announcing his association with Dura Steel.

In fact, though, neither the world at large nor Charlie Finley in particular—despite assurances from Gerst and Blue to the contrary—was buying Vida's "retirement."

"I believe Vida never had any thoughts of retiring," Finley said a few days later. "Baseball is his first and only love, and I'm quite certain that he wasn't serious in his announcement. I think he will be playing ball within a few days, before the season starts."

But the season didn't start, held up by a strike of all

major-league ballplayers over contributions to their
pension fund. And a few days before the strike began,
Vida Blue was holding another press conference, this
time to announce that he had signed to appear in the
next edition of *Shaft* movies—a series of films featuring a black detective that had met with financial and
critical success.

But it seemed that Finley was winning the war of
nerves. After all, Finley was losing only money, while
Vida was losing both money *and* the chance to play the
game he had come to love above all other activities in
life—baseball.

"If I said I didn't miss it, it'd be telling a damn lie,"
he admitted in a moment of candor. "I've been in baseball my whole life, and I love the game. You just don't
up and say, 'I won't think about it anymore.' Yeah, I
miss it."

By now one thing was changing. As far as Vida
Blue was concerned, his stalemate with Finley was no
longer something to giggle about.

12

Also a Man

The major-league players' strike dragged on into the first week and a half of the new season, which finally started eleven days late. That it began at all was in part due to Charlie Finley's root pragmatism. Faced with economic disaster at Oakland, Finley transcended his hard-line bargaining position with Vida to lobby among the club owners in favor of the players' demands.

Once the strike was settled, Charlie O. stuck to his new role of peacemaker and tried to settle his grievances with Vida Blue. Meeting the Friday after the players' strike ended, Finley came up with a new contract offer. But the negotiations again ended without Vida's signature on a legal document.

"Agreement actually was reached after I made two concessions, and then the whole thing fell apart again

121

when Blue and his attorney, Robert Gerst, refused to endorse a statement for the news media," Finley declared after the meeting.

"So," he added, "everybody went home, and I'm going to bed."

Held under conditions of tight security, these negotiating sessions (from 2 P.M. Thursday until midnight Friday) were undoubtedly the most unusual in baseball history. Besides Blue and his attorney, and Finley and his legal aide, William G. Myers, baseball commissioner Bowie Kuhn and his counselor, Alex Hadden, were in attendance.

Kuhn, of course, had just finished playing a major role in settling the players' strike—exercising (for the first time in anyone's memory) some initiative to use the coercive powers inherent in his office. That Kuhn should now consider it his job to expedite a settlement between the A's owner and his ace pitcher was hard evidence of how important the commissioner felt Blue was to the success of major-league baseball's 1972 season.

And Kuhn left that abortive meeting angry. After all, Finley had made an offer that Blue was prepared to accept: $50,000 in salary; $8,000 for a four-year scholarship at the university of Blue's choice; and a $5,000 bonus for Blue's performance in 1971. Why then had there been no agreement? According to Kuhn, because of the stubbornness of Charlie O.

"They were unable to reach accord on whether the deal should be published in detail," said Kuhn. "Blue did not want the terms released. Finley wanted to release all the terms. On this point they could not reach agreement."

Kuhn said that another meeting had been scheduled. Then he added, "I am ruling that the offer that has been made will remain in effect." And if Finley refused to renew his $63,000 offer? "I'm ordering him," Kuhn replied abruptly.

Meanwhile, the man who had first focused the public's attention on the disparity between what Vida earned and what he contributed to the ball club was again speaking out on the deadlock. During a barbecue dinner at the ranch home of Treasury Secretary John B. Connally, President Richard Nixon suggested that Charlie O. accept the contract terms dictated by his holdout pitcher.

Calling Vida "a fine young man," and pointing out that the left-hander was underpaid in 1971, Nixon added: "He has so much talent, maybe Finley ought to pay."

But the most influential argument in the eyes of Charlie O. sprang from neither the advice of the President nor the demands of the commissioner. A shrewd businessman, Finley had never been one to opt for principle over profits—particularly where no moral issue was involved. The dispute with Vida, in Finley's eyes, had been strictly about money. And money was now his prime consideration—dollars lost by the spectacular southpaw's absence from Oakland's starting rotation. By the second week of the season the A's had slipped to second place in the American League West, and it seemed doubtful that Oakland could win the pennant without Blue.

And throughout the major leagues attendance was low—particularly in Oakland. Without a gate attraction, the prospects for the A's in terms of pennants *and* finances seemed dismal.

There was pressure on Vida to sign, too. A one-year leave of absence from baseball might mean the end of his career. Besides, there were rumblings from his own teammates, who had for the most part sided with him initially, but now saw their play-off chances evaporating if Vida continued to hold out.

There also was sage counsel from other quarters. Met ace Tom Seaver said, "I feel sorry for Vida. He's a great talent, and I thought he did right to hold out. But then I decided, after Finley offered him fifty thousand dollars, that he was getting bad legal advice. He should sign, for his own good. If he has another great year, he'll be in a better bargaining position. Right now, by not pitching, he's hurting himself."

The Chicago Cubs' 1971 National League Cy Young Award winner, Ferguson Jenkins, reached the same conclusion. "Vida Blue," he said, "is the best thing that's happened to baseball in the past one hundred years. Last season the American League hitters just couldn't cope with him, so he's worth what he's asking for, all right. But," Fergie added, "I think Vida's making a mistake by asking for it *now*. If it was me, I would have come back, pitched another great season, and then demanded *double* the money he's asking for now."

Two weeks after the season began, Finley and Blue succumbed. In the office of American League president Joe Cronin, with Bowie Kuhn in attendance, Blue signed a contract for 1972 guaranteeing him $63,000 for one year, prorated from April 27. Both parties stated their satisfaction, but the next day Vida sang the blues to reporters.

"Finley," he said, with undisguised bitterness, "treated me like a colored boy."

That afternoon, at 4 P.M., Vida walked into the Oakland Athletics' dressing room. Pitchers Darold Knowles and Catfish Hunter were playing "pitch" in one corner of the clubhouse with Curt Blefary and coach Vern Hoscheit. Vida took one step into the room, then stopped and folded his arms, his lips curving in a tentative smile.

The A's kept on playing, their eyes deliberately focused away from Vida. The tension was electric.

"Glad to be back?" a reporter asked him.

"I don't know, I don't know," Vida replied. Then he went over to the trainer's table and sat down on the edge. Nodding toward the A's two-tone uniforms, he said, "Don't like the uniforms, hate that two-tone stuff."

Still the four A's in the corner concentrated on their game of "pitch." So Vida stood up, hesitating momentarily, and walked over to them. "Curt," he said, offering his hand, then proceeded to reintroduce himself to the others. When Sal Bando (who had consistently sided with Finley in the dispute over Vida's contract) entered the room, Vida immediately went over to him and greeted him like a long-lost friend. "Mr. Bando," he exclaimed with a broad grin, and the two ballplayers shook hands.

As Vida moved away to talk to other teammates, Bando watched him, saying, "It's going to be interesting. He was a good kid until the end last year, and then something happened the way he was talking. It's going to be interesting."

No more interesting than the tone of Bando's voice. Despite his misgivings, there was a new note of respect. According to Gerst, Finley had doubted Vida's courage; he had predicted Vida's total surrender. But agree or disagree with him, Vida *had* marched to his own unique drummer.

"He was a good kid last year . . ." Bando had commented, implying at the same time that he could no longer deal with Vida at that level of father to son. For Vida had bucked the Establishment and hadn't lost. And in doing so, he had created a precedent for black ballplayers as historic as Jackie Robinson's shattering of the color bar.

"I may be a *pitcher*," Vida seemed to be telling the world, "but I am also a *man*."

was done while we were already into the season," the A's manager concluded.

At the ball park, overall the season was a flop for Vida. But like the rest of us, athletes have an existence independent of the jobs they do for money. We, the fans, go to a ball park to escape the routineness of our daily lives. We may go once a week, once a month, once a year—but we expect our heroes to produce a peak performance every time. We forget that what is a special occasion for us is merely "just another day" for them. The half dozen games we attend are embedded indelibly in our memories. But a baseball player on a World Series-bound club is going to dress for almost 200 games over a season. "When your name comes up in the rotation, you pitch," Vida once said, summing up the players' philosophy that no one game, no one season are the "ultimate."

And the truth is, although Vida was struggling on the mound, outside the ball park he was learning lessons that only losing can teach. Defeat was a brutal taskmaster, but it was only through defeat that Vida would lay the mental foundation for his comeback season of 1973.

"In a way," he said later, "it was to my advantage to have the good year and the bad year back to back, because I learned so much. How people react and how people are. How people won't accept you as soon as they see there's no glory to get from saying, 'By the way, just by the way, *Vida Blue* is coming over for dinner tonight. . . .' "

His experience that year, he said, is aptly captured by the lyrics of an old twelve-bar blues. "You know that song that says, 'Nobody wants you when you're down and out'?" he asked. Then added softly, "Well, they don't be lying. . . ."

Vida was down—statistically, emotionally, an apparent failure at the age of twenty-three. Not more than halfway through that 1972 season, and the rumors that had proliferated throughout American League clubhouses were being frozen into facts—in print, in the daily columns of sportswriters nationwide. Vida had lost more than his popularity with the fans, the pundits were claiming. He had lost his fast ball, too. He was spoiled, was another assessment. The fame of the good year had gone to his head. The fame had murdered the "desire." He had been more lucky than talented, anyway, his worst critics suggested. Even by the end of his fabulous '71 season, they argued, hitters around the league were getting wise to his stale assortment of pitches: Fast ball high, fast ball low, interspersed with an occasional breaking ball that floated home on a prayer.

Vida was down, all right—in the ranking of American League pitchers, in the hearts of the fans who'd invested their dollars in him a year ago, in the estimation of the sportswriters whose job it was to explain his sudden ineptitude. But Vida wasn't *out*. To everyone else, his season might seem like a fatal waste. But to Vida, the off-year was a unique opportunity to learn the lessons winner had never taught him.

"While you find out that a lot of people you thought

were friends weren't," Vida said at the end of the 1973 season, after he had regained his superstatus with a fine 20-9 record, "you do find out that you have some real friends, after all. I learned I really did have some true friends. When I was twenty-four and eight, they were right there. When I was six and ten, they were still with me. How do I know a friend? A friend is someone who invites me to dinner on Tuesday and isn't still talking about it on Friday. A friend is someone who says, 'Right on,' when you say, 'Hey, I'll buy this round.'

"But this thing with 'friends' wasn't so much a problem with me as it might have been for someone else in my situation," he added. "For some reason, the ability comes natural to me to make a snap judgment about people and determine if they're real. Any person that comes through that door right now," he insisted, pointing to the door of the visitors' locker room at Baltimore's Memorial Stadium, "we can just pass words and I can tell you if they're for real or not. If he comes in and his eyes are big, he's starstruck, y'know? Or if he comes in and says, 'Hi, my name is Jack Jones and I work for the BLAH record company, here's my business card . . .' then I know I'm dealing with a phony, someone who wants to use me."

I had talked to him the day before, in the lobby of the hotel where the Oakland A's were staying, but our conversation didn't last more than a minute. It was the day before the opening game of the 1973 American League play-offs, Oakland versus Baltimore. Vida had already completed his great comeback year, his second season as a 20-game winner. I wanted to see what changes, if any, experience had seared into his character.

About four o'clock I spotted him, walking alone toward the reception desk—red shirt, brown slacks, but no trace of the trademark blue that had trumpeted his name during his phenomenal first season. I approached him. I reminded him that I'd be spending time with him tomorrow, after the game, in preparation for an article in Sport magazine.

"Well, you better get to me fast," he said, " 'cause when that game is over, I'm on leave. I take off that uniform. I put on my civvies. I go underground, I disappear."

His aggressiveness had startled me. "Don't worry, I won't bother you till then," I said.

And then he had smiled, that familiar Vida Blue smile, the one he gave you and me when he advertised Janssen swimsuits, the one he gave Bob Hope for Christmas in Vietnam, the one he gave Richard Nixon at the White House, while he wrestled the President's stiff grip into a black soul shake. But this time the smile was a decoy, a feint setting me up for the impact of his words.

"Bother *me?* What makes you think I'd *let* you bother me?"

He turned his back. He walked away.

My suspicion that the Fall had left psychic scars even a 20-9 season couldn't heal was confirmed the next morning. On the field, before he began his warm-ups, Vida was lecturing a group of newsmen. His theme: baseball is a business, with Vida posing as a dyed-in-the-wood bureaucrat, for whom any occasion was simply routine.

"When your name comes up in the rotation," he was telling them, "you pitch. It doesn't matter if it's here, or in Boston with that great green wall, or anywhere." And then the sarcasm penetrated. "Palmer [Orioles 20-game winner, Jim Palmer] says he's going to pitch tight to one guy, keep it down and away to another guy," he added. "Me? I just try to throw strikes."

Vida Blue was putting the press on. Vida Blue, the 1973 version, couldn't rely on simply throwing strikes. Now Vida varied his speeds, used deception as well as smoke. He had to. If in 1973 he won 20 games without the *fanfare* of 1971, he also won them without the *fast ball* of 1971.

Unfortunately, the curve he threw the writers was the best one he threw all day. His fast ball sailed high; his slider broke late. Worst of all, he had no luck. After two-thirds of an inning, with two men on base, Oriole designated hitter Tommy Davis—the same Tommy Davis who had roomed with Vida at Oakland during Vida's super year—blooped a single into right field, sending the Orioles into the lead and—moments later —Vida to the showers. The Orioles, behind starting pitcher Jim Palmer, won, 6–0.

I had arranged to meet Vida that evening. Returning to the hotel after dinner, I telephoned his room. He had been beaten badly. For the fourth time in his brief career, he had failed in a championship game.

(By the end of the A's victorious 1973 World Series, that total would swell to seven.) Despite his postgame nonchalance that afternoon in the locker room, I felt pretty sure that the defeat had troubled and embarrassed him. So I pictured him sitting in his room, alone— the way I had seen him sit alone throughout the 6-10 crisis season of 1972. I imagined him psyching himself, glaring at defeat the way a Pete Rose stares down a pitcher on a three and two count. . . .

But Vida was writing his own script.

"This is the Angel Mangual Happiness Office, Vice-President Vida Blue speaking," he answered, a woman's soft laughter in the background.

"Vida," I said, "how about getting together?"

"Not now, dude," he said in his silky, sly, out-of-uniform voice, "y' see, I got company, *fee*-male company."

Vida had learned to take defeat in stride—and keep striding forward in spite of it.

"You know, even those tough negotiations with Finley, the holdout that cost me the good year in 1972— it taught me something," Vida said. "I was just trying to get more money, for what I thought I was right in. But it was played up as if I was out to buck the Establishment, as if that was my reason. My demands were never argued on the basis of whether I deserved the money or not, 'cause in order to stop you, the Establishment makes some kind of doomsday play out of the whole thing.

"So the whole thing wasn't argued out on the real issue—money—but on a phony issue: the effect on baseball, the reserve clause, all kinds of moral issues that don't have anything, in my mind, to do with the issue of should a man get paid what he deserves.

"In the end, I learned this. When management wants to hold back giving you something, they are gonna make it look as if the fate of the whole game of baseball hangs on their decision.

"Of course, I also learned something about what agents and lawyers can do for you, and some of the things they can't," he added. "From now on, I'll be doing my own thing. Some folks think that I'm wrong to try to go it on my own. They're thinking: 'How can a young kid out of a tiny place like Mansfield, Louisiana, hope to compete with management?' Well, I don't go along with the feeling that just because a dude comes from a small town, he has to be dumb. A lot of great people come from small towns—not just baseball players, but businessmen, teachers, doctors, lawyers. Looking back on it, I think I might have done just as well without advice as I did with it. I learned a lot through all the wheeling and dealing that went on while I was holding out. My lawyer did what he thought was right, but there were times when I was disturbed about what he was doing. That's why I think I may go it on my own next time."

It was 11 A.M., in the A's locker room, three hours before the second play-off game against Baltimore. Oakland was a game behind, but no one looked worried. The A's don't get tense about baseball. In fact, playing baseball is a therapeutic relief from their interminable bickering with one another, with manager

Williams, with owner Finley. Before the team came East, for example, Angel Mangual, Vida's roommate; had issued a play-me-or-trade-me ultimatum to Williams—at the top of his lungs, in front of the Oakland press corps. And then reserve infielder Ted Kubiak's wife had been shunted to standby status because owner Finley had reserved fifteen seats for his friends on the A's charter flight.

Kubiak's wife eventually got a seat, but only—in the opinion of a number of A's—because Charlie Finley didn't *have* fifteen friends.

Charlie Finley: the extravagant enigma. A year before, when the A's had hosted the World Series against the Cincinnati Reds, Finley had had lobsters flown in from Maine for the newspapermen in attendance. Having flattered their stomachs, he then proceeded to offend their egos by bringing his mule, Charlie O., into the World Series Hospitality Suite. Many a good appetite was spoiled when a long black snout hooked itself over a newsman's shoulder and began nibbling at his salad.

Incensed by the presence of this four-legged intruder, the writers appealed to commissioner Bowie Kuhn, who ordered the mule barred from the Hospitality Suite. In 1973, when the Series was again held in Oakland, the writers almost unanimously boycotted Finley's Hospitality Suite, preferring to buy their own dinners (which meant letting their editors pay) at Oakland's most expensive restaurants. But Finley was undaunted. Finley was determined to prove he was still the unchallenged grand master of one-upmanship.

After the Saturday Series game, a number of base-ball writers were dining at Oakland's exclusive Elegant Farmer Restaurant in Jack London Square. Suddenly, in walked Charlie O. and Charlie O.—the man and the mule, plus the mule's keeper. Passing the writers' table, the mule's swishing tail knocked over a drink, staining a writer's suit. Up to then, the writer had been "pro Finley." Since then, he has joined the multitude of Finley critics.

But to balance those who see him as a bull in a china shop, Finley's friends and admirers are among the most loyal anywhere. They appreciate his boldness, taking the Kansas City Athletics and moving them lock, stock, and franchise to Oakland, when almost everyone else thought the move was financial suicide. His admirers respect his flare for showmanship, too: He introduced orange baseballs in Kansas City; he convinced Vida Blue to use a glove that matched his surname; he thought up a Bald Headed Day and Mustache Night and painted second base green, in honor of the A's in-fielder who guarded it. And he lured fans to the ball park in the early years by hiring topless waitresses as bat girls, one of whom regularly attempted to brush off an umpire or a coach's uniform while sweeping a dusty third base bag.

Unfortunately, the ranks of his admirers become thinner every year. The season he signed, Vida Blue was among them. Now his name is firmly entrenched among that long roll call of detractors. At the 1973 World Series, Vida happened to be in an elevator that was taking Finley to the lobby of their hotel. Finley gave Vida his broadest, most generous smile, and said: "Come into the hospitality room for a drink."

"I drink only milk," Vida replied.

"We have plain or homogenized," Finley said.

"I drink only chocolate," Vida replied, and turned away.

But in all his years as a headline-grabbing spotlight seeker, if there was ever an incident calculated to incite his critics, it was Finleys treatment of utility infielder Mike Andrews in that '73 World Series versus the New York Mets.

Andrews, who had played for Dick Williams at Boston, was purchased by the A's during their pennant drive. Inserted in a crucial World Series game, Andrews made an error at second base that cost the A's a victory. Immediately after the game, Finley let it be known that Andrews had been placed on the "injured-reserved" list and would not see action during the rest of the Series. Andrews flew home to Boston. He left chaos behind him in Oakland.

None of the A's believed the "injury" story, telling reporters every chance they got that Finley had pressured the second baseman into signing a phony statement, as punishment for his crucial miscue. Eventually, Andrews was recalled, at the prompting of commissioner Bowie Kuhn, impelled by the threat of a strike by the Oakland A's if Finley's action wasn't rescinded.

Mike returned as a hero. Charlie Finley subsequently was dunned with a $7,000 fine by the commissioner's office. (Other Finley offenses included turning the Oakland Stadium lights on in the bottom half of an inning, instead of the top half as the rule dictates, in order to give his club an unfair advantage etc.). But in the end, Finley was the winner again. At the end of the Series, Andrews was put on waivers. Bowie Kuhn's determination evaporated, and Finley's fine was reduced to pin money.

But in one sense, Finley's scheming did backfire. Even before Oakland finished beating the New York Mets in the World Series, word was circulating that, win or lose, this would be Dick Williams' last season with the Oakland A's. Williams was determined to quit.

Of course, when Williams' formal announcement of resignation did come, under the hot TV lights, in the jubilant Oakland dressing room after the A's had won the deciding game of the Series, he exempted—like any good soldier would—owner Charlie Finley from any blame in making his sojourn in Oakland less than idyllic.

"My resignation has nothing to do with my relations with the ownership," he said, astonishing the assembled newsmen, who knew his resignation *only* had to do with Finley. "My association with Mr. Finley has been extremely enjoyable. He never told me who to play and who not to play. He went out and bought me players when I needed them. He thought I did a marvelous job."

The newsmen handled this incredible about-face delicately in their dispatches that day, preferring to "understand Williams' embarrassing situation" or to damn his hyprocrisy obliquely, through the subtle use of sarcasm. Only Reggie Jackson was prepared to call a lie a lie. According to Oakland columnist John Robertson, Reggie gave this version of events:

"About ten days before the season ended, Jackson was plagued with hamstring problems. Because he was close enough to catch Willie Stargell for the major-league RBIs crown, he asked Williams to use him just as a designated pinch-hitter. Deron Johnson [the regular designated hitter] wasn't hitting anyway, and Reggie could run well enough to hobble around the bases.

" 'Fine with me,' said Williams.

"Then the manager made the mistake of mentioning it to Charlie O. Remember how Dick said that Finley 'never told me who to play and who not to play'?

"Well, Finley applied the veto and told Williams he was not to use Jackson. More RBIs could be too costly at contract time. Williams was so incensed he wanted to quit on the spot, but Reggie Jackson talked him out of it. Who says so? Reggie Jackson.

"Then, there was the Mike Andrews incident. Did Charlie O. not interfere there?

" 'No,' Williams lied yesterday. 'He did not.' "

Charlie Finley: the team poltergeist; an erratic force capable of propelling Mike Epstein to Texas, Ted Kubiak to Distraction, a healthy Mike Andrews onto the Disabled List, and Vida Blue to a senseless holdout that probably cost the A's at least fourteen victories in 1972.

"Wherever I go, reporters have a standard opening," Vida said when I spoke to him during the '73 play-offs. " 'Vida,' " he mimicked in a pompous baritone, " 'how's Mr. Finley?'

energy. The day is seventy-two hours long, and you've punched out till the fourth day dawns.

"The first half of this season," he replied, "I was telling people the fast ball was on vacation. And it *was*. I kept my back bent, my toes curled, my fingers the right way on the ball—just the way they teach you in the instructional books. But some days it was there, some days it wasn't."

"That first year you were getting by strictly on your fast ball," I commented.

"Well, nobody knew me," he replied. "Before the rest of the league realized who I was and what I was throwing, I had won ten in a row," he added emphatically. "And I just breezed in there for only fourteen more!"

When did he really start trying to perfect the other pitches in his armory?"

"At the end of 1971 I went back and picked up where I'd left off in the minors," he said, pulling on his low-cut spikes, tying them, then stamping the concrete floor a couple of times, like a football player battering his shoulder pads against a teammate's to get them settled. "I was tired as hell. I was still throwing hard, but I was tired. So I started working harder on the breaking pitch.

"But what I did in '71 that's different from what I do now is that then I was throwing, instead of pitching. You take Jim Palmer," he said. "Palmer's a *pitcher,* not a thrower. He has a good curve ball, a live fast ball, and a straight change-up. And that's three pitches he can use in any given situation. Whereas in '71, on three and oh, they knew I was gonna throw the fast ball. But now I've started to throw the breaking pitches anywhere, anytime, to any batter.

"You just can't stand out there and throw fast balls all the time," Vida added. "No matter how hard you throw the ball, sooner or later the hitters are going to catch up with you. You have to have something else to offer, and when you do, you have to be a better pitcher.

"Now that doesn't mean I'm going to give up the fast ball. That's still my big pitch. But as long as the hitters know I have a curve, slider, and change-up, they have to be guessing. That gives me the edge, and when the pitcher has the edge, he is going to win some ball games."

If he had the additional pitches well-perfected at the start of the 1973 season, why did he have so much trouble in his first few games?

"My first couple of ball games," he replied, shaking his head to punctuate his disgust with his own performance, "they were just bad. And then there were so many open dates on the schedule. We were going in a three-man rotation. Odom and Catfish Hunter were going real good, and my turns just seemed to coincide with the open dates. So I'd miss my turns, they'd get theirs.

"Then I had fluid on my knee," he added, "and I missed a few more starts because of that. My whole first half of 1973 was just one long march, y'know? And then I started winning."

At the All-Star break, Vida was 9–5, with a 3.53 earned run average. His record of 82 strikeouts in 145⅓ innings was below his 1971 average of nearly a strikeout per inning (301 in 312 innings), but still respectable.

"And this time, no one really took notice of my winning," he said, "which was a good thing, meaning less pressure for me. Pressure from the press, I mean. Once you've won twenty games, you're a marked man. The press is on you, day and night, at the ball park and at home. And the fans can put pressure on you, too. Fans are funny. Even though on his everyday job the eggman might drop a crate of eggs or the milkman might shatter a bottle or two of milk and think nothing about it, when the eggman and the milkman show up at the ball park, they want perfection. I drop my crate of eggs —say, I give up a couple of homers—and in their eyes I become a bum. If you're a hitter, they expect you to go four for four every time they turn up at the ball park. If you're a pitcher and a batter leads off an inning with a triple, you gotta strike out the side or they're not happy. They come to be entertained.

"But I'm a man, see? And baseball's no dream for me, it's my nine-to-five reality. So whether I pitch a no-hitter or two-thirds of an inning, it's a business, just a business. And businesswise, my attitude toward the fans is: When I'm wearing that uniform, they can boo me, call me any name they want to. But when I take off that uniform, when I become a civilian, they better treat me with respect. On the field, the fans can shout obscenities until their throats run dry. But when I get into my civvies, it's a whole new game. When I'm in my civvies, and someone comes up to me and says, 'Hey, Vida Blue, I saw you pitch yesterday, and I think you're just a [BLEEP],' then, baby, he better watch out. It ain't gonna be fan talkin' to pitcher at a ball park. It's gonna be man to man, one on one, y'dig? There ain't nobody gonna mess with me when I'm down in the street."

The change of attitude — from naïve, innocent dreamer to tough, hard-nosed pragmatist—was not accomplished without fundamental changes in Vida's life-style, too.

"I just made up my mind I was going to live differently than before. So, beginning in 1972, one of the main things I decided was this. I made a new rule for myself: Don't take nothin' for free, 'cause, as the proverb goes, there ain't nothin' you get in life that you don't pay for somehow," Vida said, slipping—as he does when he wants to draw irony out of an anecdote or blood out of a critic—into the black vernacular. "I decided I wasn't going to take a free car from all those dealers who were offering them to me. I decided that I didn't want anybody to give me anything when I walked into a store. I got myself an American Express Card, a Master Charge card. It may sound small, but it was a beginning.

"For instance, in early '72, during my holdout, some of the local merchants around Oakland got together and said they'd make up the difference between what Finley was offering me and what I was asking for, out of their own pockets. And I said no. No way. The fact is, they were probably doing it strictly from the standpoint of getting publicity. But even if they were sincere, I wouldn't take it. First, I felt I should get the money from the people whose pockets I was enriching with my performances. Second, I decided it wasn't right to get something for nothing."

His friends have changed, too. The losing season eroded the fair-weather acquaintances, and to the hard core of friends from 1971 that remained, Vida has added another group.

"Now I spend a lot of time out at Berkeley [the University of California campus, and a spawning ground of the counter culture]. I walk the streets in my blue jeans, with my white sailor cap, with my shades. I have friends over there—friends who don't put me through any changes, who aren't always asking for my autograph, who never hand me their business cards. My first year," he added, "I let everyone climb on my bandwagon. This year I was the driver of the wagon again, but didn't nobody ride on it but me."

Then Vida started telling me about a former fan club member he'd visited in hospital three consecutive days before the team flew to Baltimore—one of those factual, but contrived, anecdotes ballplayers feed writers to sanctify their public images.

"I went there to see a kid who got shot in the eye coming home from school. He was a member of the fan club that I had, which we broke up before the beginning of the '72 season. They wanted me to meet with the members every so often, and I didn't have time . . . well, I had the time. The truth is, I didn't want to give the time. It was a forty-five-mile-drive, round trip, and I guess the members became disinterested 'cause I never showed up.

"In any case, I went to see the kid three days in a row . . . ."

Halfway through the story, he stopped, grinned, and said, "Hell, why should I lie? The real truth is, the *first* day I really went to see the kid. The next *two* days I went to see the nurses."

In fact, though, Vida does have an abiding interest in kids. But unlike most ballplayers, he doesn't attempt to translate this concern into cash for himself. Many ballplayers, with an uncanny sixth sense that tells them when the eye of the media is focused in their direction, will sign autographs and turn up for clinics and kiss their junior fans like old-style machine politicians campaigning for reelection. Vida's contacts with kids are spontaneous and unpublicized. He has fun and is after nothing more. He doesn't convert kids into commodities he can capitalize on as "image builders."

"I have always wanted to get a sports car," he told me. We were walking out of the clubhouse now, down the narrow, damp tunnel that leads under the stands, into the dugout, then up a few steps, onto the playing field. He had told me that he owned a medium-priced pontiac sedan, but that his dream was to own a Mercedes two-seater.

"Why not buy it now?" I had asked. "You're a bachelor. "You're making sixty-three thousand dollars.

There are a lot of ballplayers making less money who have Mercedes two-seater sports cars."

"Yeah, but see, I got all these kids with me all the time," he replied. "I cruise out on a Sunday morning, and I find a local park, and the first thing I know the car is full of kids. I take them home, I let them hang out for the day, listening to my records. They're mostly black kids, and they're real good for me to be around once in a while. Y'see, they don't put me on any pedestal. And I've learned too much about pedestals ever to get put on one again by anyone, kid or adult. People put you on a pedestal only so that later they can knock you off."

In football season, Vida says he can usually be found—on days when he isn't at the ball park—at a local high school, where he relieves his own youthful football fantasies by practicing with the varsity. "But they don't let me play quarterback," he said. "Instead, they use me to work out the quarterbacks, shagging down passes as a wide receiver."

His other main interest—besides shooting an occasional game of pool and apart from the women who naturally flock after a very, very eligible bachelor who earns $63,000 per annum—is music.

"I listen to all kinds," he said. "Especially groups like the Temptations, vocalists like Curtis Mayfield and Eddie Kendrick. Just a week ago, I got a whole new speaker system, for my brand-new two-bedroom luxury apartment. I have four speakers in my living room, two in one bedroom, two in the other—eight speakers in all. I have all my speakers hooked up; I have plenty of music taped. The only thing is, I had the thing for a week and didn't have the courage to really turn the system up, to get the volume I paid all that money for. See, I've been keeping it real low, to avoid getting complaints from the neighbors. But when I do turn that thing up, to where I like it, believe me: I'll be able to hear it when I'm on the road in New York!"

Outside, behind the batting cage, before that second game of the 1973 American League play-offs, Oriole-designated hitter Tommy Davis—whose single had been the decisive blow against Vida the day before—was chatting with a couple of teammates. The irony is, Davis had been Vida's roommate at Oakland during the 1971 season. Later their relationship had cooled, and the day before, when they bumped into each other near the batting cage, you could hear the icicles shatter. Today, however, Vida strode over to Davis and grabbed a bat out of Tommy's hands. Flailing it, his arms rubbery, Vida said, "This is what you looked like when you got that lucky hit off me, y'know? Man, you keep that up, next year they'll *designate* you down to a girls' softball league."

Davis roared with laughter. Vida did, too. Instantaneously, he had thawed a frigid relationship. But the new Vida Blue—as he has proved by the changes in his life-style, in his code of ethics, in his head—would rather be called candid than charming.

In fact, only one thing about Vida Blue has *not* changed over the past two years, and that's his style of pitching. Vida admits his fast ball doesn't rocket quite the way it did in 1971, but he argues: "I think I throw as hard *consistently*. My average fast ball is just as hard as the average one in 1971." And despite the development of the curve and slider (he calls the combination a "slurve"), he insists, "My style is still to go right at the batter. Even on the days when I don't have the good fast ball, I'll beat you with what I have. My game is to go strength for strength. If you like that low fast ball, inside, I'm gonna give you the fast ball right in on your hands. If you like it right over the plate, I'm gonna throw it over the plate and tailing away. Most of the time I'll be right there, giving you what you think you like and teaching you not to like it.

"You see," he added, "I was losing ballgames in '72, but I didn't lose my determination. That's why the twenty games I won this year mean more to me than the twenty-four I won the first year. The first year no one knew what was going on till I was seventeen and three. This year they were laying for me. They were on me from the beginning.

"I did it, I won twenty. A lot of people said I couldn't do it; some people even said I was washed up, through for good, that I'd thrown my arm out. Well, I showed them. And more important, I showed myself."

It was only a half hour before game time now. Fans around the A's dugout were clamoring for Vida's autograph—naïve, star-struck preteens who didn't know that baseball was a business.

"Gotta sign for them," Vida said, "gotta do it for the kids."

"It's kind of sad," I said, as we walked toward the

fans shouting "Vida, Vida" and waving their pens and their programs.

"What's sad?" Vida asked.

"Being Vida Blue," I replied. "Being a superstar and twenty-four, but without a dream."

Vida stopped. He took an imaginary snap from center. He dropped back. He threw an invisible touchdown pass, calling: "I *know* I could still play some football!"

Index

Aaron, Henry, 80–83
Ali, Muhammad, 129
Allen, Dick, 127
Alou, Felipe, 57
American League, 132; All-Star Game, 78–83; 1971 play-off, 96, 101–5
Anderson, Sparky, 83
Andrews, Mike, 140–42
Aparicio, Luis, 82
Arizona Instructional League, 31–32

Bahnsen, Stan, 44–45
Baldwin, Clarence, 15–16
Baltimore Orioles, 71–73, 101–5, 133, 135
Bando, Sal, 43, 45, 68, 87-88, 93, 108–9, 126, 130
Bauer, Hank, 41, 44–45
Bench, Johnny, 82
Berra, Yogi, 42
Birmingham, Alabama, Class AA baseball, 38–42, 46, 47, 49
Blair, Paul, 104
Blefary, Curt, 78, 125–126

Blue, Sallie (mother), 10, 24, 31, 53, 76
Blue, Vida: awards: Cy Young, 107, Most Valuable Player, 71, 108; birth, 10; "black Johnny Unitas" dream, 9, 14, 17, 24 ff.; Blue Sunday, 92; Blue Tuesday, 75; childhood, 10–16; college football offers, 25; college scholarship clause, 143–44; curve ball, 36, 39, 47, 147–48, 155; first major-league game; 42 ff.; high school sports, 9 ff.; 13, 16–23, 27; interview, 134–156; joins Athletics, 31; minor leagues, 32–41, 51–54; name, 10 ff., 75, 86, 120; 1971 All-Star Game, 78–83; 1971 season, 64–105; 1972 season, 127–133; 1973 season, 132–36; pitching record, 32, 34, 41, 46, 47, 52, 62, 74, 77, 90, 107 ff., 149; pitching technique, 23, 38, 39, 40, 46, 98 ff., 130, 135, 147 ff., 154 ff.; pressure, 84, 85 ff., 95 ff., 102, 104, 145, 149; publicity, 92, 120;

157

retirement announced, 118 ff.; salary negotiations, 108–25, 136 f., 142; Vida Day, 76; Vietnam tour, 115; White House guest, 69

Blue, Vida, Sr. (father), 10, 24, 28

"Bogartin," 86

Booker T. Washington High School football team, 21

Bosman, Dick, 68

Boston Red Sox, 45, 63, 65, 67, 74, 91

Boyd, Don, 40

Burlington Bees, Class A baseball, 33 ff., 40, 48 f.

California Angels, 41–44, 45, 71, 76, 78, 94

Campaneris, Campi, 57 ff.

Carew, Rod, 57, 82

Casanova, Paul, 69

Cater, Danny, 45

Cedeno, Cesar, 52

Chance, Dean, 107

Chicago White Sox, 50, 54–56, 71, 89, 94

Cincinnati Reds, 129

Clemente, Roberto, 81

Cleveland Indians, 71, 88

Crider, Jerry, 56

Cullen, Tim, 94

Cronin, Joe, 81, 125

Cy Young Award, 106–8

Davis, Tommy, 78, 103, 106, 117–18, 135, 154

DeSoto High School, 9, 15–18, 20, 21–23, 27, 29

Detroit Tigers, 46, 71, 88

Dick Cavett Show, 92

DiMaggio, Joe, 42

Dobson, Chuck, 66–67

Doby, Larry, 13

Duncan, Dave, 73

Dura Steel Co., 118–19

Ellis, Dock, 80, 83

Epstein, Earl, 119

Epstein, Mike, 68, 142

Feller, Bob, 82, 92

Fingers, Rollie, 56, 68

Finley, Charles O., 27; career, 28–29; 30, 41, 47, 49, 61–64, 70, 76; relations with Blue, 86; 1971 play-off, 101–2; players' strike, 121; fined, 140–41; World Series, 138–39, 142–45

Flood, Curt, 113

Ford, Whitey, 84

Freehan, Bill, 71, 83

Garr, Ralph

Gerst, Robert, 108, 111–17, 119, 122, 126, 128

Gibson, Bob, 115, 128

Grambling College, 13, 25

Harrah, Toby, 68

Hendrick, George, 34

Hope, Bob, 115

Horlen, Joel, 55–56, 89

Horton, Willie, 71

Hoscheit, Vern, 78, 125

Houk, Ralph, 77, 80

Hunter, Jim "Catfish," 67, 86, 95–96, 125, 148

Iowa Oaks Class AAA baseball, 49–51, 53–54

Jackson, Reggie, 43, 45, 63, 83, 96, 100, 108, 116, 141–42 145–46

Jacobs, Lee, 15, 16

Jenkins, Ferguson, 107, 115, 124

Johnson, Deron, 142

Jones, Stan, 35

Kaline, Al, 46–47, 71–72

Kansas City Athletics, 139

Kansas City Royals, 56, 69, 73, 76, 88

Killebrew, Harmon, 57, 60

Knowles, Darold, 92, 125

Koufax, Sandy, 79, 80, 97; compared with Blue, 98–99, 116, 128
Kubiak, Ted, 138, 142
Kuhn, Bowie, 122–23, 125, 138, 140–41

Little League, 14, 15
Locker, Bob, 57
Lolich, Mickey, 107
Lopat, Ernie, 42
Louisiana Interscholastic Athletic & Literary Organization (LIA-LO), 17, 37
Love, Bob, 13

Mangual, Angel, 136, 138, 143
Mansfield, La., 10 ff., 15, 22 ff., 30, 33 ff., 106, 116, 137
Mantle, Mickey, 42
Marichal, Juan, 115
Maris, Roger, 43, 97
Mays, Willie, 81, 82
McAuliffe, Dick, 71
McDowell, Sam, 80, 89
McLain, Denny, 74, 85, 91, 97
McNally, Dave, 96, 103 f., 115
McNamara, John, 62, 64, 70
Melton, Bill, 89
Messersmith, Andy, 42
Milwaukee Brewers, 57, 69, 73, 100
Mincher, Don, 94
Minnesota Twins, 57 ff., 66, 73, 75 f., 94
Minor-league baseball, 36–38, 49, 51, 52 ff.
Monday, Rick, 94
Most Valuable Player Award, 108
Motton, Curt, 105
Murcer, Bobby, 145

National Football League (NFL), 13, 25, 28
National League, All-Star Game, 80–83
New York Mets, 140–41
New York Yankees, 42–45, 75, 92

Niarhos, Gus, 40
Nixon, Richard, 68 f., 91, 93 ff., 123

Oakland, California, 28, 139
Oakland Athletics, 33, 42, 47, 53, 57, 62 ff., American League West title (1971), 94; attendance, 77, 97, 110 ff.; pitching staff, 66, 71, 73; play-offs (1971), 101 ff., (1973), 133 ff., 137; World Series (1972), 129 ff., (1973), 140 ff.
Oakland Black Caucus, 117
Odom, Johnny Lee, 66 ff., 145, 148
Oliva, Tony, 57

Palmer, Jim, 72, 115, 135, 147
Perry, Gaylord, 115
Perry, Jim, 57 ff., 73, 115
Peters, Gary, 91
Pizarro, Juan, 49 ff.
Posedel, Bill, 78, 99
Powell, Boog, 73, 105

Raschi, Vic, 42
Reserve clause, 111, 113, 115
Rettenmund, Merv, 105
Reynolds, Allie, 42
Rigney, Bill, 61
Riley, Pat, 56
Robinson, Brooks, 82, 87
Robinson, Frank, 73, 83, 105
Robinson, Jackie, 13, 126
Rodriguez Aurelio, 43
Roland, Johnny, 53
Rose, Pete, 136
Rudi, Joe, 57

Sain, Johnny, 90
Sanford, Jack, 27
Seaver, Tom, 107, 115, 124
Seghi, Phil, 49
Segui, Diego, 68
Shantz, Bobby, 90
Siebert, Sonny, 91 ff.